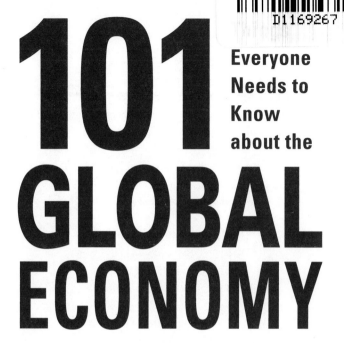

101

Everyone Needs to Know about the

GLOBAL ECONOMY

The Guide to Understanding
International Finance,
World Markets, and
How They Can Affect
Your Financial Future

Michael Taillard, PhD

Aadamsmedia

AVON, MASSACHUSETTS

Published by Adams Media, a division of F+W Media, Inc.
57 Littlefield Street, Avon, MA 02322. U.S.A.
www.adamsmedia.com

ISBN 10: 1-4405-4411-5
ISBN 13: 978-1-4405-4411-8
eISBN 10: 1-4405-4511-1
eISBN 13: 978-1-4405-4511-5

Printed in the United States of America.

10 9 8 7 6 5 4 3 2 1

This publication is designed to provide accurate and authoritative information with regard to the subject matter covered. It is sold with the understanding that the publisher is not engaged in rendering legal, accounting, or other
professional advice. If legal advice or other expert assistance is required, the
services of a competent professional person should be sought.
—From a *Declaration of Principles* jointly adopted by a Committee of the
American Bar Association and a Committee of Publishers and Associations

Many of the designations used by manufacturers and sellers to distinguish
their product are claimed as trademarks. Where those designations appear in
this book and F+W Media was aware of a trademark claim, the designations
have been printed with initial capital letters.

This book is available at quantity discounts for bulk purchases.
For information, please call 1-800-289-0963.

DEDICATION

This book is dedicated to my children, Dante, Gabriel, Katherine, and Amelia. It is my hope that this book will help people to make better decisions than those being made today.

Contents

CHAPTER 8. MOVEMENT OF CAPITAL . . . 185

CHAPTER 9. INTEGRATION . . . 214

CHAPTER 10. DEVELOPMENT . . . 232

INTRODUCTION

Think back to the last time you bought a car. Of course, you were interested in questions like, What kind of mileage does it get? What's its safety record? And does it come in a really cool shade of red with a bitchin' CD player?

But you also might have wondered if it was built in America. Was it from the assembly lines of the Big Three—General Motors, Ford, or Chrysler? Was it the product of American workers, or were you contributing in some small way to shipping those manufacturing jobs overseas?

These days, more and more people ask themselves questions such as these. But the reality is that the vehicle you drive, regardless of what company's name is on it, is composed of the parts and labors of many nations. It was, perhaps, assembled in Mexico, with parts from China and electronics from Taiwan, fashioned from natural resources extracted from South Africa, using engineering specifications from Germany, and fueled with oil from Saudi Arabia. In truth, almost nothing that's a part of our lives comes from only one country. These things are all interconnected in complex ways, and each international connection influences a range of things, from the amount of money you make at work to where you live. Call it the Economic Butterfly Effect. The price of rice in China really *does* influence your credit card's interest rates, but if you don't know why, there's little you can do to prepare.

Global economics studies those relationships between people of different geographic locations as they participate in economic transactions. The dynamics of the economic relationships between nations, or even between different parts of a single nation, present risks and benefits to you. The better you understand these relationships, the more successfully you'll be able to adapt to the changes that are occurring daily in your life:

everything from gas prices to your customer service experience at a department store.

The mechanisms by which these economic transactions take place and influence other transactions are varied, but they occur at every geographic and economic level. You might want to "Buy American" in the hope of saving American jobs and contributing to our national prosperity. But in truth, you might as well try to narrow yourself down to purchasing all your goods at a single store. It won't do you much good. Not only is it just about impossible, but even if you could do it, the store owner doesn't want to sell exclusively to you and no one else.

For better or worse, today we live in a global society. The world won't disappear just because you close your eyes. Instead, globalism presents us with a world of opportunities if we can see them. As Americans expand our range of possible transaction partners, the potential benefit for everyone increases.

The risks associated with globalism don't lie in trading with other countries and in buying goods that are made elsewhere. Rather, they're in being unprepared for what the world has available. When you understand how people behave in their attempts to make the best use of the planet's scarce resources, you'll have a greater understanding of how the global community affects your life and what you can do to adapt to an ever-changing world.

CHAPTER 1

The Basics

Issues in global economics are common news stories, but it's sometimes difficult to find out what any of it actually means. Even though those current events are among the most important in your life, the people who give you the news often don't know or explain how these issues will affect you.

This is why we should start with the basics. Not only is everything else in global economics built upon these fundamentals, but even these most basic principles impact our daily lives. Unless you know what you're looking for or how to properly respond, you're at the mercy of the ebb and flow of the economic tides that reach across the globe.

1. GLOBALIZATION

Globalization refers to both the increasing integration of the world's nations and the process by which that integration occurs. Although globalization is not a new concept—there are major international trade routes dating back at least as far as 2,000 B.C.—trends in technological advancements and cross-border issues have dramatically increased the degree to which far-separated locations on the earth have become interconnected, both economically and otherwise. Much of what contributes to the increased globalization is attributed, rightfully or not, to the efforts of governments as they work to coordinate agreements and treaties that facilitate these international interactions (the development of trade blocs such as the European Union, for example). The reality, however, is that globalization often occurs independent of any government policy.

Increasing globalization is inevitable; it affects all industries and all nations. What is its real cause? In a word: technology. As we make improvements in our ability to communicate instantly across long distances and more quickly transport people and cargo, our ability to take advantage of the benefits of associating with foreign nations increases. Not only have these technological advances made it faster and more convenient to buy and sell goods across the globe, but it's also cheaper because we're improving the cost efficiency of communication and transportation, as well as decreasing the risks associated with transporting goods over long distances.

Consider such new technology as the cargo jet, the computer, or even just the telephone. Because of these inventions, to place an order we no longer have to send a letter overseas (where it can easily go astray). We don't have to pay a higher price to cover the risk that the company we're buying from might lose shipments to storms or bandits.

Globalization is a fact, but like many facts, it isn't all good or all bad. For example, pollution crosses national boundaries without concern for what policies are in place to limit international trade. The airborne carbon from a Chinese coal power plant is dispersed through the global atmosphere just as easily as the ash from an Icelandic volcano or the fallout from a nuclear bomb. At the same time, research and trade in information goes on daily between nations using informal or unofficial channels.

Globalization means we can better take advantage of a greater range of markets to which we can sell our goods or from which we can purchase our supplies. Economists study and try to explain human behavior in their relations with one another.

Globalization is an inevitable result of our own attempts to maximize the value of our transactions. It has increased during the past few decades as a result of technological advances, and so has global economic interdependence.

What You Should Know

If you buy something from someone on the other side of the planet, the principles are still the same as if you were trading with someone across the street. National boundaries are artificial barriers that add complexity to our transactions (which will be discussed in later chapters), but other than the sheer distance involved, the transactions themselves are no different.

Let's pretend for a moment that you live in the 1700s. The primary modes of transportation are horse and boat, and the best method of communicating across long distances is to shout— really, really loudly—or send a handwritten letter. To purchase something from the other side of the world is a nuisance and takes a long time.

Fast-forward to the twenty-first century. It is now easier to purchase things from halfway around the globe than it was to purchase things from across a single nation in the eighteenth century, thanks primarily to our technological advances. Today, rather than sending a courier or merchant on a journey lasting many weeks or months to retrieve goods and bring them back (all the while carrying valuable money or merchandise that is liable to be damaged or stolen along the way), you make a phone call or visit a website. Within a week the item is delivered to your doorstep. People now have access to a wider variety of goods, at varying levels of quality and price, which are not always available within their own nation.

A single look in your spice cabinet tells the entire story. Three hundred years ago, your collection of spices—which in this century you most likely bought in the same store for just a few dollars each—required caravans to travel from China all the way to Greece by horse or foot along the difficult path known as the Silk Road. The trade was so profitable that despite the cost of sustaining a team of people for months, entire empires were built on the sale of goods considered to be rare or exotic (such as spices).

In the modern era, exposure to and integration with other cultures is a normal part of everyday life. There are probably a handful of ethnic restaurants or stores within a short drive from where you live. The aisles of your local supermarket display tea from China, marmalade from Scotland, matzoh from Israel, and naan and poori from India. Foreign trade has become more about cost efficiency than the availability of exotic goods. (In fact, most of these foreign goods are no longer considered especially exotic.) Despite technological advances, however, governments are no more successful at truly prohibiting or even restricting foreign trade without self-harm than they were in the eighteenth century.

Think about it this way: Imagine you live in Metropolis, which is a few miles away from Gotham City. Metropolis wants to discourage you from shopping in Gotham and keep you—and your money—in Metropolis. The city decides to put a tax on any goods you purchase from Gotham City. However, as long as prices in Gotham are still lower, even after paying the tax to Metropolis, you'll still shop there, won't you?

Even if Metropolis raised the tax so high that you decided to shop in your own city, would you benefit by paying higher prices? No. The people of Metropolis would just be paying more for their goods than necessary. Businesses that would normally buy their supplies from Gotham City are paying more for those goods, resulting in even higher prices.

In an effort to retaliate, Gotham City now institutes its own set of taxes. And now it's impossible for Metropolis to sell its own goods to the city next door. Metropolis, upping the stakes in the trade war, institutes a law that prohibits you from shopping in any other city. Does that help the businesses in your city? Of course not, because now Metropolis businesses are uncompetitive. The people of Gotham City never went away; you just stopped being able to buy from and sell to them. Instead, you have to rely on just one city from which you must purchase everything you need. Costs go up, availability goes down, and everyone is harmed in the process.

Why You Should Care

Many people think that globalization is something created by the government, that globalization is taking away jobs. They want to stop the current trends in globalization. But as we've just seen, even if you close your borders entirely, the world is still out there, with all its terrifying threats and glorious opportunities. The best thing you can do to take advantage of the opportunities and mitigate the risks is to simply be aware of what's going on around you; expand your attention globally rather than on your immediate geographic surroundings.

No matter what the circumstances, in today's world information is king. As noted, the increased trend in globalization is a result of improved technological advances, so use those advances to increase your advantages. The Internet is probably the best tool available for price and availability comparisons, as well as managing shipping and payments. There are a wide variety of companies online designed specifically to facilitate such transactions.

2. PRODUCTION POSSIBILITIES CURVE

The production possibilities curve is a graph that global economists use in their studies. It illustrates the potential combinations of the types and quantities of goods that a nation is capable of producing.

This is really pretty simple. At a given point, any nation can produce a certain amount of various types of goods in different combinations. When a nation is producing the maximum quantity of goods possible (that is, the nation is using all its production potential), this is called the production possibilities frontier because the nation can produce no additional output.

If a nation is producing the maximum amount of any particular good or service for which it has the available resources, in order to produce more it must give up resources from something else. (This is called Pareto Efficiency.) Naturally, any nation can produce less than the maximum of which it's capable, but, for trade purposes, nations try to avoid such inefficiencies (this is discussed further in topic 4, Comparative Advantage). For simplicity, global economists often discuss the production potential curve using only two different types of goods. Of course, nations produce more than just two types of goods, but the premise remains the same, no matter how many different kinds of goods are involved.

What You Should Know

The bad news is that every nation, regardless of size, has limited production potential; it can produce only a limited amount of any specific type of product or service. The good news is that each nation tends to excel in the production of a few different types of products and services. The other piece of good news is that even if your nation isn't especially good at producing something, there are other nations that excel at producing those goods and services. When a nation must give up some part of the production of one good in order to produce more of another, this is called the opportunity cost.

Let's say the only two things your nation produces are beer and pizza. You're able to produce a maximum of $100,000 of beer, but then you have no resources to produce any pizza at all. You're also able to produce $50,000 of pizzas, but then you'd have no resources to produce any beer. On average, you'd have to give up two gallons of beer just to produce one additional pizza, while you'd only have to give up one pizza to make two additional gallons of beer. That means you're using fewer resources for every gallon of beer produced than every pizza produced.

Okay so far?

Another way of looking at it is that you can produce twice as much value in beer than pizza using an equal amount of resources. The opportunity cost of producing $100,000 in beer would be $50,000 in pizza. That's what you'd be giving up in pizza to produce the maximum amount possible of beer.

Each nation has its own production possibilities curve. National growth can occur either when a nation produces at a level closer to its production possibilities frontier—in other words, it gets rid of inefficiencies—or when it expands its production possibilities frontier. In either case, the nation is producing more than it was before. Increased economic efficiency occurs when a nation:

- Produces more, using an equal amount of resources
- Produces an equivalent amount, using fewer resources
- Produces more, using fewer resources

This doesn't change the production possibilities curve directly, but it changes the quantity of different goods being produced to maximize resource usage.

Why You Should Care

The tradeoff inherent in the production possibilities curve of a nation determines the prices that a nation pays for its goods relative to other nations. If you have to use more resources to produce a good than the next nation over, the price you'll charge for that good will be higher because the cost to produce it is higher.

This is true of all transactions, not just international ones. Let's say you're a farmer who's very good at growing corn, but it takes you a very long time to make farm tools. Your neighbor is good at making farm tools but not so great at growing corn. You'll end up selling your farm tools for a higher price than your neighbor because it takes more time and effort. On the other hand, if you buy farm tools from your neighbor using the corn you grew (or at least the money you earn from selling corn), then you'll be better off. *This is why we buy and sell stuff.* Otherwise, we'd all just make everything ourselves.

The total size of a nation's production possibilities curve plays a critical role in determining which nations are large, rich, and powerful. In other words, the production possibilities curve of the nation you live in has been a large factor in your quality of life. Essentially, the nations that improved over the centuries were those that were able to harness the production potential of the natural resources available to them. These include high-yield, nutrient-dense foods that can be farmed so people have time to develop other skills, animals that can be domesticated so people can use their resources, and natural minerals from which tools and infrastructure can be built.

3. ABSOLUTE ADVANTAGE

A nation with an absolute advantage in a particular good is able to produce more of those goods using the same or a smaller amount of resources as some other nation. Often, having a lot of natural resources such as arable land, mined goods, oil, gas, or other such things is enough to give a country an absolute advantage. As long as the volume of these things exceeds the amount that is consumed domestically, the nation can sell off the surplus.

For instance, if Nation A can use 100 pounds of wheat to produce 1,000 bottles of beer and Nation B can use 100 pounds of wheat to produce 5,000 bottles of beer, Nation B has an absolute advantage over Nation A in beer production. The reasons for this may be that Nation B has a more efficient production process than Nation A and knows how to derive more beer per pound of wheat. It's also possible that labor costs in Nation B are lower so it costs less to produce a bottle of beer there.

What You Should Know

Having an absolute advantage in one good or service isn't as helpful in trade as you might think. Those nations that don't have an absolute advantage in a product will not export it because some other nation can produce the good more cheaply. Nation B in our example above may export some of its beer, but this won't last for long. As demand for Nation B beer grows, so will its price increase, including labor costs. Over time this diminishes Nation B's absolute advantage, and eventually some other nation will be able to produce beer just as cheaply as Nation B.

Why You Should Care

Relying on absolute advantage for a nation's economic health is extremely inefficient. As we saw above, absolute advantage in any product is a temporary condition that is eventually eroded by trade. So you shouldn't get too complacent, even if right now your country can produce more beer more cheaply than any-where else. Given free international trade and growing demand, it won't be that long before your six-packs are rising in price and more and more beers from other countries are showing up in your local supermarket.

4. COMPARATIVE ADVANTAGE

A nation has a comparative advantage over another nation in the production of some good or service when it has less opportunity cost. In other words, the nation has to give up fewer resources for the production of other goods in order to produce something than another nation does. This not only increases efficiency in resource usage, thereby decreasing the costs for the production of that item, but it also makes the economy as a whole more efficient in its allocation of resources.

What You Should Know

Comparative advantage is the primary basis for all sustainable international trade, and the basis for all transactions that take place within a single nation. Imagine for a moment trying to produce everything you need to survive. You have to build your own shelter, grow or hunt your own food, and so on. Alterna-tively, you can focus on making extra of whatever you're able to produce the most of, using the resources available to you and trading that surplus for everything else you need. When indi-viduals focus on developing an expertise in just a few skills and doing those very well, it's called specialization or the division of labor. When this happens on a global scale, where all the com-panies of a nation focus on performing those functions they can do well using as few resources as possible (meaning cheaply), then it's called operating within their comparative advantage. Even if a nation doesn't have an absolute advantage in anything, nations benefit by taking advantage of each other's comparative advantage.

Comparative advantage differs from absolute advantage in that it is more concerned with opportunity cost than financial cost. As we saw above, an absolute advantage tends to be a temporary state of things. Having a comparative advantage means that the nation is specializing, using its resources more efficiently, keeping costs down, and relying on other nations to produce those things that it may not be as effective at making itself.

Why You Should Care

Sometimes people forget that these issues in global economics are just a composite of what the people and companies of a nation are doing. Comparative advantage is one of those issues. When a company is "sending jobs overseas," what that actually means is that something the company used to do is a function in which your nation has a comparative disadvantage. It's now cheaper for the company to outsource that function to another nation.

Complaining about this or appealing for government protection isn't going to help anyone. If a country's competitiveness is sustained only through lawsuits and economic protection, then its increased resource use is harming the ability of other people and other companies to be competitive in the global market. This throws the entire national economy out of equilibrium.

Many individuals and companies adapt to this problem of having a comparative disadvantage. Some innovate, introducing new methods or technologies that reduce costs, improve quality, or alter the product market. Others will alter their position *within* the market: perhaps they become importers rather than producers, or focus their operations to perform only one function of the production process.

Whatever you do for a living, remember this: There's probably someone somewhere in the world working on a better, cheaper way to do it and so gaining competitive advantage.

5. GAINS FROM TRADE

Gains from trade occur when two nations exchange those goods each is capable of producing cheaply; together they produce more than each could ever hope to produce on their own. This is possible when nations rely on their relative comparative advantages. Each one produces surplus amounts of those things that can be made using fewer resources. The countries then sell these surpluses to each other. As a result of this global trade, every nation has more resources available to it.

What You Should Know

Gains from trade are only possible when the people of each nation focus on producing those things in which they have a comparative advantage while importing goods from another nation that holds a comparative advantage over them. Hark back to the beer and pizza example we used earlier. In this case, it costs two beers to produce one pizza. Conversely, it costs one pizza to produce two beers. Now let's imagine that this production is split between two nations. Here is the production of each before trade:

- Nation A: $10,000 beer and $5,000 pizza
- Nation B: $2,000 beer and $4,000 pizza

Note that Nation A has an absolute advantage in both beer and pizza (that is to say, it produces more of both than does Nation B) but Nation B has a comparative advantage in pizza. Without trade, the maximum they could produce together is $21,000 in goods. Each country is better at producing different things. If each one decides to specialize in what it's good at, allocating resources from its weaker industry to its stronger one and then trading its surplus, we can end up with gains in the total number of goods:

- Nation A: $20,000 beer and $0 pizza
- Nation B: $0 beer and $8,000 pizza

Now the two nations are producing $28,000 in total value. So when each nation produces only what each is very good at rather than attempting to produce everything, *even if one nation has an absolute advantage in everything*, they both benefit. Each of them decreases its own use of national resources, which means lower costs, more competitive business, and more sustainable growth.

Why You Should Care

Trade in this manner increases total wealth for everyone because there is a much larger total value of resources in each nation compared to the number of people. That's great news when you're talking about increasing national wealth or even creating a sustainable economy. Those nations that participate in trade increase in wealth more quickly, and a proportion of that wealth translates into a better quality of life within the nation.

6. TERMS OF TRADE

One way to measure the value of trade between nations is with a calculation called the terms of trade. The terms of trade compares the value of a nation's exports with its imports, expressed as a percentage. There are two versions of this calculation: the two-nation model and the multiple-nation model.

The two-nation model is simpler and is commonly used to explain how the terms of trade calculation works. It also provides additional information when assessing things such as the balance of payments, exchange rate, and relative business cycle fluctuations between nations (discussed in later chapters). To make this calculation, divide the total dollar value of a nation's exports by the total dollar value of its imports, and then multiply the answer by 100.

This ratio measures the value of a nation's imports and exports. So, if Brungaria exports $1,000 worth of goods to Freedonia and imports $500 worth of goods from Freedonia, then Brungaria has exports worth 50 percent more than Freedonia and Freedonia has imports worth 200 percent of those of Brungaria.

If you're thinking that it really can't be that simple, sadly, you're right. This calculation is only a starting point for figuring out the value of trade between nations. The reality of a nation's terms of trade is more complex since trade typically occurs between multiple nations, trading multiple goods, with different advantages and currency values. This is where the multiple-nation model for terms of trade becomes important. The multiple-nation model is actually one of several price-index models for trade that can account for a wider variety of import and export transactions. In a realistic scenario, these become very involved. But don't worry—I'm not going to overwhelm you with a lot of math.

What You Should Know

A nation's terms of trade is not a measure of its economic health or the competitiveness of its products in the global market. Instead, the terms of trade merely measures a ratio of total value of imports to exports. This ratio is meaningless without context. What you need to know is how you should interpret the value based on the greater context of trade balance and variations of economic cycles between nations.

Any time the terms of trade seems to contradict other trending factors for these areas of economic concern, you can reasonably assume that something else is causing the relationship. Along the same lines, if some trade issue appears to be inexplicable, measuring the terms of trade can help point you in the correct direction.

Using the terms of trade as a single indicator is like noticing a single landmark while you're on a long journey—it can tell you whether you're on the right path, but it won't replace a proper map and compass.

Why You Should Care

Organizations, individuals, and even entire nations use the terms of trade to predict fluctuations in trade, exchange rates, and economic well being. If your country has extremely high terms of trade but a particular company in which you're interested (for example, for investing purposes) is exporting little, it may indicate that the company's industry has a poor comparative advantage globally. Knowing what to expect from trade will guide decisions about how best to take advantage of foreign opportunities.

7. VARIETY VERSUS REGIONALIZATION

People like variety—but not too much. Consider some "ethnic" restaurant chains. Taco Bell isn't really Mexican food, the Chinese Buffet isn't really Chinese food, and all the fast food restaurants you can think of that have branches in China are serving items that cater to the local tastes and preferences rather than those items that originally made them famous in this country. That's where the trade-off between variety and regionalization lies—in people's desire for something different but not *too* different.

In economics, variety is typically considered to be a good thing, since diverse product offerings provide consumers with different options that appeal to many tastes while stimulating competitive innovation. The reputation in the United States of Swiss clocks, Chinese silk, Indian spices, and Italian clothing stems from the fact that different regions are able to offer better-quality products than are available domestically. People throughout the ages have desired the foreign, the new, and the exotic. In order to gain some new experience, we look to other nations . . . only to find out, quite often, that it isn't to our liking.

What You Should Know

There is an informal sliding scale for global products. On one extreme are those things that are completely familiar to us; on the other are those that are completely unfamiliar. Anyone involved in foreign trade must find a balance that optimizes personal benefit and company sales. If the company's products are too unfamiliar, violate too many taboos, or contrast with established tastes too greatly, not enough people will buy the product for the company to be competitive. If the company's products are too familiar, there is little to differentiate them from those produced by domestic companies. The goal, then, is to differentiate through their offerings without alienating their customers.

Goods and services that are in stark contrast with cultural norms, while enticing for a small percentage of customers, typically will not compete well. For example, in the United States, Chinese restaurants have a very difficult time selling traditional Chinese food (e.g., braised chicken feet) to people from a non-Chinese background. Instead, they sell such things as General Tso's Chicken (which, by the way, isn't Chinese at all) because it uses flavors and ingredients that American consumers associate with Chinese cooking.

Why You Should Care

If you're a small business owner, you may be seeking to export your goods, so it's important to understand the market you hope will be purchasing them. Is your product one that has variable traits? Even if all you do is grow rice, there are multiple types of rice, each varying in popularity and price based on the individual nation. Maybe the nation you're considering exporting to tends to prefer long-grain rice, while your company has produced only jasmine rice until now.

That brings us to the next question: Does your product line offer traits that the potential customer market will want? You might be able to sell your jasmine rice as a type of high-end foreign delicacy rice, but if the people of that nation have no recipes that use this type of rice, they still won't be interested unless you can market the recipes just as effectively as you market the rice. You need to be aware of whether or not you're applying assumptions of your own nation to people from other nations.

As an informed consumer, you need to understand the impact regionalization has on products and whether it will influence the product you are purchasing. Your expectations about the product may differ significantly from those of consumers in the product's country of origin. For years, Westerners assumed Chinese-made products were of poor quality. The reality is that the expectations for cheap manufacturing were different in China than they were in many Western nations. China had experienced decades of economic mismanagement, which forced its manufacturing methods back to a nearly pre–Industrial Revolution era. This, in combination with pressure put on manufacturers to maintain minuscule profit margins, caused a high degree of quality problems, including some unsafe goods. The situation could have been avoided had the companies performed their due diligence to ensure that the products were being made to the expectations of their target market rather than the expectations of the Chinese market.

8. ECONOMIES OF SCALE

When a company can produce something more cheaply per unit by increasing quantities, we say it's creating economies of scale. Think of it like a bulk discount, but on a much larger scale: when a company sells more of a product it's able to charge a lower price for it. This happens for two primary reasons:

1. Increased efficiency in the usage of available resources (internal economies of scale)
2. Lower per-unit cost of supplies when purchased in large volume (external economies of scale)

Internal economies of scale mean a company is more efficiently using its assets. Let's say a company owns one factory and one machine to produce its products. The machine produces 250 units per month. The company improves its machine to the point that it can now produce up to 500 units of the product. However, the cost of maintaining the factory each month hasn't changed; the only increase in cost has been the supplies put into the machine to make the products. So, if the company increases the number of products its machine is making, the average cost per product for the company decreases since the company is now making more products without changing the monthly cost of the factory. Look at it this way:

$$\text{Cost of Factory} = \$1{,}000 \text{ per month}$$
$$\text{Cost of Unit of Product} = \$10$$
$$\text{Making 250 units} = (250 \times 10) + 1{,}000 = \$3{,}500; \text{ Average cost}$$
$$= 3{,}500/250 = \$14 \text{ per unit}$$
$$\text{Making 500 units} = (500 \times 10) + 1{,}000 = \$6{,}000; \text{ Average cost}$$
$$= 6{,}000/500 = \$12 \text{ per unit}$$

If the company buys a larger machine, able to produce 1,000 units, it can reduce its costs even more. Of course, if the company only has enough warehouse room to store 500 units, then it's paying for a larger machine but can still only produce a maximum of 500 units. At this point, the ability to produce more units increases the average cost, causing *diseconomies* of scale.

External economies of scale occur when a company is able to purchase supplies in large volumes. If a company grows so large that it needs more supplies than other companies can provide without increasing production costs, this creates diseconomies of scale.

What You Should Know

Going global greatly improves an organization's potential to achieve economies of scale. That's often a primary motivation behind a company's desire to expand internationally.

As the price of an individual product increases, the demand for that product will go down. While there are some exceptions to that rule, it holds relatively constant. Now, consider the inverse of that. An organization's sales have stopped growing, so it actually spends money to increase its production capacity. Why? The company's executives know that by purchasing equipment that can produce a much higher quantity of goods, the company can charge a lower price for them. The lower price attracts people who previously couldn't afford their products as well as people who were previously customers of higher-priced competitors. In this way, economies of scale sometimes result in a "natural monopoly," whereby a single company gains control of a particular market by making its goods cheaper.

All of this increases with the global expansion of an organization's operations: The potential for internal economies of scale increases as the total number of potential customers grows; and the potential for external economies of scale increases as organizations expand the total number of suppliers globally competing for their business.

Why You Should Care

Improved globalization has allowed organizations to take advantage of a larger customer base and a greater number of suppliers, decreasing costs and improving operating efficiency. This has allowed organizations not only to attract customers with lower incomes, creating a customer base where one did not exist before, but also to compete with those from foreign nations hoping to enter the local market. The bottom line is that when a company achieves economies of scale through globalization, you benefit.

9. ECONOMIES OF AGGLOMERATION

When a company's operations are geographically closer to its suppliers, customers, partners, or even unrelated organizations and competitors, it can experience cost savings; these are called economies of agglomeration.

What You Should Know

People move to be near their jobs, while organizations move to be near their customers, suppliers, and partners. As a result, everyone benefits from the group's ability to efficiently specialize its operations, create synergy, and even stimulate bargaining between competitors.

Being near suppliers and customers also allows organizations to more effectively respond to changes in the demand for their products. Even when competitors are located near to each other, the costs of distribution for mutual suppliers is reduced, and both organizations can attract a wider number of competing suppliers.

Why You Should Care

Nothing stays constant, so you need to pay attention to trends. Where people are locating, where organizations are setting up shop, what people are buying—all these things are very important in global economics. Something as simple as placing some of your financial assets in a nation with lower investment taxes can make a large difference.

10. LOCALIZATION

Although it's counterintuitive, dramatically increasing levels of globalization are actually bringing about a new form of localization. In order to fully integrate and improve their competitiveness in foreign markets, global companies treat every nation in which they have customers as their home country. Today there are four categories of companies:

1. *Domestic.* These companies work within a single nation, sourcing their supplies from within it and selling to customers only within that country. This includes companies that purchase goods from local companies that were manufactured abroad.

2. *International.* An international company is headquartered in a single nation, but has import or export operations that give it a presence in other nations. This category includes companies that sell their products online and ship internationally.

3. *Multinational.* A multinational corporation is one that has a physical presence in multiple nations. The firm may actually own a foreign branch, might have a foreign partnership, may have foreign investments, or could have any number of other forms of arrangements in place that give it full or partial ownership over international functions.

4. *Global/Transnational.* Global companies are those that lack a home nation. They keep multiple points of control at different locations on the planet in order to stay responsive to the local markets. They often offer stock in several different nations, have geographically diverse management, and sometimes even lack a single formal headquarters. This is done so that each market receives specialized attention and the units of the company that

are concerned with a regional market can give that market their full attention.

Notice that as a company progresses from a domestic firm to a global one, it expands its offering of goods to the world that were originally meant to attract domestic customers. Organizations tend to gradually integrate themselves into foreign markets, so that the pinnacle of organizational global reach becomes total market integration rather than merely global reach of sales. This is the nature of localization.

What You Should Know

The phrase "Think globally, act locally," attributed to town planner and social activist Patrick Geddes, perfectly captures the idea of localization. Even the largest of international companies can remain successful by maintaining a cohesive, coordinated organization that is as diverse as its customers. In this manner, it remains a single global entity that meets the varying needs of local communities, both in its product portfolio and its ability to maintain a local presence and more effectively manage operations.

As already noted in topic 7, Variety Versus Regionalization, organizations of all sorts try to be as responsive as possible to local tastes and trends. For instance, in those nations that have a primarily Muslim population, the Red Cross changed its name to the Red Crescent, the crescent being a commonly used symbol from the Islamic religion. The organization still provides the same basic services, but it changed its image slightly to accommodate the needs of the local region. In order to manage a product portfolio that is diverse enough to remain competitive on a global level, and to continuously manage that portfolio to keep up with changing trends and ideas globally, each region is often given a certain degree of autonomy to respond to localized needs.

The concept of localization also extends to the operations of the company. Global and multinational organizations tend to disperse their management and core operations across a wide geographic region. In the past, a company would send individuals or entire departments to live abroad, sometimes for years at a time. They found that this wasn't entirely economical; nor was it entirely effective. Foreigners attempting to work in another nation, particularly as managers, often have a difficult time relating to the local people. So the trend has changed to hiring local people and maintaining at least one individual from each nation in which the organization has a presence in executive management or on the board of directors.

Sometimes localization is required by the laws of the nation in which a company operates. It is not uncommon for a government to stipulate that an organization operating within its borders must hire a minimum percentage of locals and invest locally. These types of regulations are motivated by a desire to stimulate economic growth within the nation, though they limit a company's ability to manage its earnings.

Why You Should Care

As a result of globalization, many organizations are changing to better reflect the culture and ideas of the world's population rather than those of their home nation. Global economics is composed of far more small businesses than huge ones, and operating globally is often not so very different from operating domestically.

Consider a single Chinese family that farms pearls from oysters and sells them to tourists. One tourist recognizes the opportunity to purchase the pearls cheaply in bulk and develops a close relationship with the family. Later he forms a company and distributes catalogues of pearl jewelry in his home nation of the United States. This company owns no actual factory, has a staff of only six people, and sells retail jewelry at wholesale prices across the entire United States. It's an international company. It takes advantage of comparative advantage and economies of scale, and although it operates globally, it thinks locally. This is the best face of global economics.

CHAPTER 2

Organizations of Global Economics

They are huge and influential. They produce ominous-sounding research and refer to data that few people actually see and to experts whom few people actually meet. They hold closed-door conversations and broker deals among leaders in world politics, business, and the intellectual and cultural elite.

It all sounds very secretive, as if shadow societies of faceless organizations are manipulating worldwide economic events. Commentators have speculated that these organizations are exploiting entire nations of people for the benefit of a handful of individuals. Is there a basis for this? Do these international organizations, which contribute so greatly to the influences of the global economy, truly hide in the dark corners of the world, plotting the exploitation of the world's population?

The short answer is no. Much of the confusion surrounding the organizations of global economics results not only from the sheer size and volume of their operations, but from their language, which can be incomprehensible to all but a select few.

This chapter will describe the biggest and most important organizations in global economics, including their original missions, how they've evolved over time, how they help, how they can be harmful, and (most importantly) how they influence your day-to-day life.

11. WORLD TRADE ORGANIZATION

After World War II, there was—understandably—a very strong awareness among people and governments around the world about international cooperation, coordination, and communication. Discussions were held concerning economic cooperation and integration, which set rules for the interaction of nations and their people both in peacetime and in war. Organizations were formed, and many of the most advanced industrial nations determined an interest in maintaining a global presence and actively participating in the world community. Perhaps not all nations were on good terms with each other—the Cold War effectively began in 1947—but every nation now understood the importance of establishing some universally accepted set of principles that the world should respect and by which each should abide.

One of the largest, most influential, and most successful of the organizations that evolved from the discussions of this period was the World Trade Organization (WTO). The WTO was formally convened in 1995, but its origins lie in a series of treaties called the General Agreement on Tariffs and Trade (GATT) that was established after World War II. Any nation that agreed to the terms of GATT would increasingly decrease trade restrictions, eliminate a huge proportion of tariffs, and promote free trade. The 1986 round of GATT talks laid the foundations of the WTO as an organization to promote and facilitate the goals of GATT, to provide a forum for member nations to discuss issues in trade, to enforce GATT and WTO rules for member nations, and to resolve disputes that arise between member nations.

To date, the WTO has been highly successful at achieving its goals, and 157 nations in the world maintain active membership in it.

What You Should Know

The primary function of the WTO is to increase free trade between nations. It does this by requiring member nations to adhere to certain rules; member nations are entitled to certain benefits and guaranteed equal treatment by other members. There are five broad principles by which the WTO operates:

1. *Nondiscrimination.* All member nations of the WTO and their products must be treated equally.
2. *Free Trade.* Over decades, negotiations by WTO nations have removed billions of dollars worth of tariffs and trade restrictions. WTO member nations continue to work toward removing barriers to trade, increasing the free movement of people and capital across international borders, and increasing economic integration.
3. *Predictability.* Nations that agree to the terms of the WTO and to any other economic agreements within the WTO forum also agree that their agreement is binding. They will allow transparency so that others can easily see that each nation is upholding their part of the agreement.
4. *Fair Competition.* In addition to free trade, the WTO also requires fair trade. Fair trade means that nations adhere to rules that do not allow for predatory business practices.
5. *Encouraging Development.* Those richer WTO member nations and the WTO itself contribute expertise and encouragement to smaller, poorer, and less-developed nations. While the organization doesn't provide loans or other forms of direct involvement, these nations are often given additional time to make the economic transitions required by WTO regulations.

Why You Should Care

The WTO sets the guiding principles and acts as the intermediary for the vast majority of international trade. The negotiations that resulted in GATT and the WTO dramatically increased the volume and value of trade, reducing costs of tariffs and other barriers to trade, encouraging imports and exports rather than economic isolation. Since the majority of all nations in the world are WTO members, including the largest economies in the world, any time an economic conflict arises (which is frequently) between these nations, the WTO must negotiate a resolution. The WTO does, in fact, have the ability to bind nations to penalties, fines, and corrective measures. If the offending nation does not adhere to the rules or decisions of the WTO, its membership can be revoked.

12. WORLD BANK

Started in 1945, the World Bank is, as one might expect from its name, a bank for nations. It provides loans, facilitates exchanges and transactions, generates interest, and performs other banking functions. Today the World Bank actually consists of five different organizations.

1. *International Bank for Reconstruction and Development.* This bank lends money to nations for the purposes of infrastructure development. The first loan was issued to France for reconstruction after World War II, but the scope of loans has expanded to assist with any form of infrastructure construction for the purposes of national economic development.

2. *International Development Association.* This bank also lends
    money for the purposes of development, but rather than
    infrastructure construction, this bank lends money to very
    poor nations to use in making available to their people things
    such as medical care, schools, utilities, and other basics of life.

3. *International Finance Corporation.* This organization is less
    a bank and more a financial advisory firm. Rather than
    lending, it offers investment services, financial advisory
    services, and asset management services to governments
    and the private sector in order to help stimulate private-
    sector development in least-developed nations.

4. *Multilateral Investment Guarantee Agency.* Since poorer
    nations hold greater risk for investors in the form of
    political volatility, this branch of the World Bank insures
    private investors against such risk to help attract more
    investments. Rather than all forms of investment, how-
    ever, the agency insures only new investments that will
    have an impact on the nation's development.

5. *International Centre for Settlement of Investment Disputes.* The
    name of this particular branch of the World Bank pretty
    much says it all; this branch provides locations and arbitration
    services for the member nations of the World Bank.

What You Should Know

All the organizations of the World Bank require borrowing
nations and organizations to undergo evaluation and maintain
cooperation with the World Bank to ensure that their use of
funds is responsible and that they take positive steps toward economic reform. This has done two things:

1. It has helped many nations take positive steps toward
    achieving sustainable development and economic growth.

2.   It has attracted a lot of criticism and conspiracy theories about the actual intent of organizations that lend money in return for political reform.

It is widely accepted that the World Bank has improved its success rate for lending programs that develop into sustainable programs and pay back their loans. Still, that rate is only about 30 percent. What about the failures?

In some cases, there have been economic shocks as the huge influx of investment creates volatility to which many impoverished nations can't adjust. In others, there has been little stable economic and infrastructure growth, and poor nations find themselves with a debt they cannot repay. This has led many to believe the hidden intent of the World Bank is to gain control over poor nations for the benefit of richer countries.

Why You Should Care

The World Bank is funded by its member nations. You should judge its success based on whether the bank creates global economic benefit equal to or greater than the cost of sustaining it. As noted, it has improved in its success rate, which is promising, and the work it does is very important. But unless the bank can prove that it can continue to improve its success rate and actually stimulate national development in struggling nations, then that will put the legitimacy of all five of the World Bank institutions into question.

13. INTERNATIONAL MONETARY FUND

The International Monetary Fund (IMF) was first established at the Bretton Woods Conference in 1944 and began operations in

1945. Its goal was, and still is, to monitor the economic conditions of its member nations and take steps to prevent avoidable and short-term economic crises. Originally that meant managing the fixed-exchange-rate policy between nations (that is no longer applicable since the majority of nations now use floating currencies) and helping to rebalance nations' current accounts in their balance of payments. However, it no longer performs either of these functions.

Today the IMF still closely monitors the economies of its member nations, providing information and data to the other nations to help each coordinate their domestic and international economic policies. The IMF works with nations to provide technical assistance in the areas of fiscal and monetary policy, increasing trade and economic integration, attracting investment, and banking. In extreme cases, the IMF will provide loans to those nations that are experiencing a short-term crisis.

As with the World Bank, the IMF has attracted a significant degree of controversy as a result of requiring political reforms for borrowing nations. The IMF has also come under fire for a number of other problems, specifically multiple backfired attempts at development in the areas of food, medicine, the environment, free trade, and human rights. Still, the IMF insists that its successes outweigh its failures.

What You Should Know

The IMF has been criticized by external sources as well as many of its own economists for adopting a growth-at-all-costs policy. Many also claim that adherence to the conditions set on loans issued by the IMF have led to epidemics of diseases such as tuberculosis and HIV, extensive damage to the environment, poor management of food production, and other harm. IMF, critics say, starts from the idea that all economic sectors should be industrialized and that manufacturing for the sake of outsourcing should be done, regardless of the secondary harm caused. That philosophy extends to several of their economic policy recommendations. Their methods of currency devaluation to attract exports and decreasing investment and economic stimulus during times of economic crisis have proven to be extremely harmful to the global economy.

The IMF states that its role in the global economy is more important and beneficial than any mistakes it's made along the way. To back this claim, it points out that it has significantly helped several nations in South America minimize the impact of economic mismanagement and helped other nations privatize their industries and move away from closed or state-controlled economies.

Why You Should Care

There's a saying: "Never trust a person giving you investing tips." To a large extent, that's true of the IMF. Some countries have concluded that while the IMF can provide a useful service, many of its policies and economic ideas are out of date and flawed. Since the IMF only works with governments, how can this possibly influence you?

Well, everyone in the world is under the control of one government or another, and those governments will influence your life. Whether you and others around you benefit from IMF involvement through a stronger and more stable economy will depend on how economically savvy are your nation's leaders.

14. ORGANISATION FOR ECONOMIC CO-OPERATION AND DEVELOPMENT

The Organisation for Economic Co-operation and Development (OECD) was begun in 1948 to create a cooperative effort among European nations to rebuild after the destruction of World War II. Then, in 1961, it was reorganized with broader and more abstract goals intended to promote free trade, economic development, and international cooperation. It does this by working cooperatively with governments and private companies from around the world, making recommendations and developing policies for nations (nonbinding, of course, but often implemented or otherwise taken into consideration by member nations). It publishes books, data and statistics, reference guides, research studies, and economic performance data. The OECD derives a large portion of its authority from its expertise and professionalism.

What You Should Know

The OECD covers a wide range of topics, from energy to trade to business and unions. Every subject in global economics is studied by the OECD. That is where its activities end, however. The organization studies, researches, and makes recommendations. Its only method of pushing organizations, public or private, to take action is by supporting its position with well-founded research. Its role is academic, aimed at understanding the economic forces at work and suggesting ways to optimize them for the benefit of member nations.

Why You Should Care

You should care about the OECD for the same reasons that governments care about it: It's one of the most respected authorities on global economic issues in the world. The recommendations it makes are taken seriously by nations during the formulation and implementation of economic policies. The OECD's information will have an influence on the role of your nation in the greater global economy, which in turn will affect your daily life.

15. ORGANIZATION OF PETROLEUM EXPORTING COUNTRIES

Oil has been among the most important commodities in the world since the early twentieth century. For a long time the vast majority of oil production was confined to just a handful of nations. In 1960, many of these nations formed an organization called the Organization of Petroleum Exporting Countries, or OPEC, which now has twelve member nations collectively producing 33.3 million barrels of oil per day. The goals of OPEC are to represent the interests of its member nations and the oil industry, as well as to stabilize price and production of oil in a manner that optimizes wealth for its members.

What You Should Know

OPEC is an oligopoly—a cartel. That means that its members do not compete with each other. Instead, they cooperate to maintain a guaranteed higher price for their product. This cartel is less powerful now than formerly, as huge reserves of oil have been found in non-OPEC nations, but to a large extent OPEC's behavior has already shaped the price and operations of the world's oil industry, and still influences them today. OPEC has refused to acknowledge that their reserves are being depleted quite quickly and that oil's high price has encouraged innovation in alternative energy sources (a free competitive market would, of course, lessen the drive toward innovation, since oil prices would be lower).

OPEC's members include (in alphabetical order): Algeria, Angola, Ecuador, Iran, Iraq, Kuwait, Libya, Nigeria, Qatar, Saudi Arabia, the United Arab Emirates, and Venezuela. Many of these nations rely exclusively on the oil industry to sustain their economy, and many are politically or socially unsettled. In some instances OPEC has refused to export oil to nations; in other cases, oil production facilities have been attacked to disrupt supply. Since oil is critical to the health of the global economy, this volatility makes many nations around the world nervous.

Why You Should Care

The entire economy of nearly every nation on earth relies on oil. Without it, the economies of the world would effectively come to a stop. Ensuring the ready supply of oil is among the most critical objectives for global economics.

16. GOVERNMENTS

Every citizen of every country is subject to a government. Governments maintain control over all the activities of the people and organizations within their borders and represent those people and organizations when interacting with foreign governments. They vary quite a bit in their degree of control over the people of their nation, as well as their source of power.

- *Degree of Control.* This ranges from attempts to maintain total control over all actions and thoughts of a citizenry to a guarantee of complete freedom to pursue whatever actions each citizen wants. The former extreme is usually described as a totalitarian government, while the latter is described colloquially as a free society.

- *Source of Control.* Some governments take control by force—say, through the use of military or mercenary forces—while others are granted control by popular vote. There are many intermediate points between these extremes.

Generally speaking, economics should have very little to do with governments and politics. Economic relations emanate from human behavior as people work to optimize the distribution of limited resources. As a result, the forces that govern economic transactions are natural behaviors that have nothing to do with the government in power—unless that government establishes control over some aspect of the economy.

What You Should Know

Government policies most directly related to the global economy are those that affect trade and the movement of capital or people across international borders. These specifically define what types of transactions the people and organizations within a nation are allowed to participate in with people outside the same nation.

In addition to those policies established to directly influence the role of a particular nation and its citizens in the global economy, domestic economic policies also have a more indirect influence. Monetary policies can change the quantity and value of money by altering printing and distribution of a currency and changing interest rates. In addition, fiscal policies manage taxation.

Why You Should Care

Companies around the world are competing to supply you with goods and services. To what degree you have access to them depends on government policies—both those of other nations and your own.

The economic forces in each nation and between nations influence the economies of other nations, and because of this, people around the world are becoming increasingly interconnected. As a result, governments increasingly interact with each other in matters of economics. How well two governments relate to each other and are able to get along will determine, to a large degree, the amount of trade that each government will allow with the other nation.

17. NONGOVERNMENTAL ORGANIZATIONS

When an international organization isn't a branch of government, a collection of governments, or a profit-seeking company, it's called a nongovernmental organization (NGO). These organizations don't fit into any other category. They often act like government agencies, but they aren't directly associated with any government. They act like corporations, but their goal is not to generate revenues.

You've probably heard of many NGOs without being aware that they fall into this category. The Red Cross, for example, is an NGO. The International Organization for Standardization, the organization that develops the standards by which many companies operate, is also an NGO. So are the World Wildlife Fund (WWF), the Peace Corps, and even the Wikimedia Foundation (the people who bring you Wikipedia). All these organizations have three things in common:

1. They maintain global operations.
2. They are autonomous from any government (though many NGOs receive contributions from governments).
3. They operate without anticipation of revenues in exchange for their contributions.

Well, you might think, it sounds as if NGOs are just charities. While it's true that many charities are NGOs, that's not the case with all of them. Nor are all NGOs charities. NGOs fall into three primary categories:

1. *Charities.* These are organizations whose primary intent is to provide services to people in need of assistance. Examples include Doctors Without Borders and Oxfam.
2. *Professional.* These are organizations whose primary intent is to regulate, coordinate, and promote a specific field or profession. Examples include W3C (World Wide Web Consortium) and BNI.
3. *Political.* These are organizations whose primary intent is to influence governments, usually focused on a single and narrow range of topics. Examples include Human Rights Watch and Transparency International.

A large number of NGOs cross multiple categories—for instance, Amnesty International. Others don't fall into any single category.

What You Should Know
The ultimate goal of each NGO is to help bring stable growth and development to the nations in which they operate. While some seek to improve the quality of life through specific issues (medicine, environment, human rights, etc.), others attempt to

standardize industries through the dissemination of information, improved production methods, and coordination and representation that allow for safer and more informed transactions.

It is the goal of NGOs to change the market environment rather than the market itself. The context in which economic transactions take place is the real focus of NGOs. They all play a role in shaping the nature and role of the organizations of the global economy.

Why You Should Care

Since NGOs don't directly participate in the global economy, they are sometimes seen as peripheral, but that couldn't be further from the truth. Not only do these massive organizations control a large volume of assets—all purchased from different companies and different nations from around the world, thereby exerting economic influence through trade—but they also play a strong role in shaping public opinion and government policy. NGOs work closely alongside government agencies, even often being the recipients of government funding, to achieve their goals.

18. MULTINATIONAL COMPANIES

Multinational companies have operations in multiple nations. These operations can be of varying complexity, ranging from simple import/export at one extreme to multiple headquarters and staffs at the other. What makes multinational companies (MNCs) different from other companies is that, over the centuries, firms have increased to a size unprecedented in history. They command a volume and value of assets unheard of before our era, and they are often sought after by government agencies for consulting roles on policy questions.

MNCs are one of the primary inhabitants of the global economy. Not only are they by far the most significant supplier of goods and services, driving the production of a nation as they work to meet the needs of their customers, but collectively they also represent the primary source of employment and manage the vast majority of the movement of capital and goods around the world. Customers are, of course, the counterpart to companies; customers represent "demand" while companies represent "supply."

What You Should Know

The primary role of companies is to produce the goods and services for which people are willing to pay money. The ultimate goal of a company is to improve its financial performance by cutting costs, increasing revenues, and performing operations more efficiently. International trade and investment, as we've seen, help this process.

Why You Should Care

For our purposes, all businesses are multinational businesses in the sense that they all have an influence on global economics. As such, they intimately connect us to the world and impact every aspect of our lives. It can be easy to become overwhelmed by the immense size and operations of a multinational company; in fact, MNCs, at their heart, are simple entities that exist for one reason, and one reason only: to make a profit.

19. G8 SUMMIT

Welcome to the world's most exclusive club: the G8 summit. Not officially an organization, the G8 is a collection of eight of the ten largest nations in the world, measured by gross domestic product (GDP). The eight meet for an annual summit to discuss topics of global concern such as trade, climate change, energy, and other issues in global economics.

Although the G8 is just a forum for representatives from these nations to talk, their regular interactions, ability to make and commit to decisions during the summits, and follow-up on the subjects discussed make the G8 summit more durable and give it more sustained influence than originally intended.

The nations began meeting in 1975 as the Group of Six, or G6, and included France, Germany, Italy, Japan, the United Kingdom, and the United States. Later they added two nations, Canada and Russia, making them the G8. The G8 includes only the largest and most developed economies in the world. China and Brazil, although within those top economies, are not included, and the European Union is represented but does not hold a chair at the summits.

The G8 does not have a permanent office or administration. The meeting location and office of president rotate every year among the different member nations. The exact goals and subjects discussed at the summit vary depending on the political goals of the individual member nations. Although fluid, the topics are always focused on large global issues that require a unified effort among multiple nations. Although there is no obligation to come to an agreement on any particular issue during the summit, the aim is to discuss these economic questions and come to a consensus on how to move forward.

What You Should Know

Agreements and treaties aren't required from the G8 summit, but it is politically useful for the leaders of the member nations to show that they are making progress on pressing issues and that they can work together to form a consensus on how to resolve the problems. Those issues not readily resolved are often followed up on by smaller meetings to work out the details and logistics.

At the thirty-eighth G8 summit in 2012 participants agreed to the following:

- *Energy and Climate Change.* Member nations agreed to pursue more aggressive transitions to renewable energy, to reduce the use of fossil fuels for environmental purposes, and to reduce the economic volatility associated with shocks in the price and supply of oil.
- *Food Security.* The G8 nations formed what they called a "new alliance" with the nations of Africa to help develop an infrastructure for agricultural production and distribution intended to hold off starvation and reduce the number of people living in poverty by approximately 50 million.
- *Middle East Development.* Participants agreed to financially support the Arab Spring and work toward reducing political and social volatility in the region.

Not all of these items refer to agreements and alliances, but this forum allows the decision-makers of each nation to freely communicate on these problems in a single location with the purpose of setting goals.

Why You Should Care

Just because it's unlikely that you'll participate in the G8 summit, don't think that you don't play a role in the topics addressed and the actions taken by those representing your nation. These people are politicians, and their ultimate incentive is self-serving. Issues that are important during an upcoming election are the ones that will be given the most attention at the meeting. The impact the G8 summit has on the global economy should be obvious. The largest nations in the world by economic size work to find resolutions to the biggest economic problems of the era. The exact influence, however, will depend on the subjects that are addressed.

CHAPTER 3

Balance of Payments

Exports leave one country and imports enter another country; ownership of capital assets is exchanged time and again across the globe. All of this happens in varying quantities and prices, and for each nation it is recorded and added up in a huge record called the balance of payments.

The balance of payments, often referred to as the BoP, is a detailed accounting of the value of all international transactions for a country. It is broken down into three primary elements: the *current account*, the *capital account*, and the *transfer payments account*. The transactions relevant to each account are then further classified according to the type of goods or services being exchanged.

1. The **current account** includes all imports and exports of goods and services. Within the current account are such categories as manufactured and assembled goods, and services.

2. The **capital account** includes all transfers of capital ownership. Within the capital account are reserve assets, foreign direct investment, and any other form of ownership stake that a foreign nation might hold in another country's economic well-being.

3. The **transfer payments account** deals with those transactions in which goods or capital are given freely to others without compensation. This account is sometimes referred to as the balancing account.

The primary principle of the balance of payments is that it must always (as the name implies) balance. This happens through a process similar to double-entry accounting: Each international transaction influences the value of two BoP accounts for each nation. Any time one of the accounts in the balance of payments changes value, a different account changes in value *by the same amount but in the opposite direction.* For example, if the current account increases by $35 million, then one of the two remaining accounts (capital or transfer payments) must decrease by $35 million.

On a smaller scale, of course, this happens in any transaction. For instance, when you buy a $35 bottle of gin, you receive the gin bottle in what would be a current account transaction. You now possess a bottle of gin that increases by $35 your net worth in goods. You give the store owner $35 in cash, a capital account transaction (you're effectively transferring some of your capital to the liquor store owner) that decreases your available capital by $35. If, by some miracle, the store owner decides to simply give you the gin, then the transaction represents a decrease in the transfer payments account and an increase in your current account, thus balancing the BoP (this is the reason the transfer payments account is sometimes called the balancing account).

The exact values of a country's three accounts don't really matter as much as the overall health of its economy. This is despite the fact that economic commentators use the term "imbalance" to describe any current account that has a value other than zero. (Keep in mind that a current account with a value of zero would require a nation to export exactly as much as it imports. This *never* occurs, even among the most isolated nations in the world.) The only important thing about the BoP is that the total, when you add up the values of all the accounts, must equal zero. It's not important that any single account should equal zero.

The balance of payments is used, primarily, to keep track of transactions that take place internationally. It helps guide economic activities for governments and organizations in a given nation. The information provided by the balance of payments is critical to understanding and projecting a nation's competitiveness in the trade of products from particular sectors. It also helps in managing and estimating movements in exchange rates and evaluating the overall health of the economy, particularly when used in the context of domestic inflationary and unemployment rates. Understanding the volume and types of transactions and investments that take place within a nation is a bit like finding the edge piece of a puzzle: It's a great way to get an idea of what the overall picture will look like.

20. CURRENT ACCOUNT

When people think of measuring trade, they are usually just thinking of the current account. This, as I explained previously, is the portion of the balance of payments that measures the value of goods and services being imported into and exported from a nation. Think of your own country; odds are that it both imports and exports goods and services. Exports *add* value to the current account, while imports *subtract* value from it.

Goods are those things that have a physical form. They may include consumer goods, such as Italian-made cars or Japanese electronics (that is, products directly used by consumers). They can also include business capital goods such as machinery (that is, products that are used to produce other products). Or they can include raw materials such as steel or coal.

Services are actions for which people or organizations are paid. They provide value to the customer but no physical product. Common services that are traded internationally include transportation, research, medical procedures, research, and teaching. These things all provide value to people in other countries and must, therefore, be recorded on the balance of payments as contributing to the value of the current account.

A decrease in the current account is almost always associated with an increase in the capital account (discussed further in topic 21, Capital Account), and vice versa. This is in the nature of current account transactions, which, more likely than not, infer cash transfers in the other direction. In other words, if you buy something, the company from which you purchase it will usually want to get paid in cash, even if that company happens to be halfway across the world.

What You Should Know

If you've ever shipped a package or even mailed an envelope internationally, you filled out a form about the type of goods being shipped, their value, and a number of other pieces of information that the customs officials in a nation will want to know before they allow such a package to enter their country. These forms are a primary source of information for the government agencies that track such things about goods that are coming in and out of your country. Services, since they often do not require shipment, are a bit trickier to track.

This tracking system with its multiple forms isn't always entirely accurate. For instance, small companies and individuals tend to report lower values or prices on goods they're exporting in order to avoid being charged a tariff (a tax on imports) by the government of the country they're shipping to. Government tracking of imports and exports applies to everyone, no matter how big or small their shipment, when they transfer goods between nations.

Governments can somewhat compensate for the deviation on estimated values of imports or exports by using other measures, such as those used with services. Services use mostly tax statements for tracking. If you work overseas, you're probably aware that there's a portion on your U.S. tax forms that asks about foreign income. The government also measures the number of people who enter the country, where they're staying (whether with family or not, geographic locations, etc.), and how long they stay. Companies that ship or receive goods from overseas track these shipments as well, both for management purposes and, quite often, for tax purposes.

The information derived from the current account is, by itself, very limited. Since changes in the balance of payments always affect two accounts, looking exclusively at the current account doesn't tell us much. However, a positive or negative balance, particularly if it has an extremely high value, can provide some information about the health of the economy. Used in conjunction with the capital account, information derived from the current account can help project future changes in a nation's trade, and even help identify some of the broad sectors that are influenced by trade in order to infer those industries in which a nation has either an advantage or disadvantage.

Why You Should Care

The degree to which a nation imports less than it exports can tell you critical details about the sources of domestic unemployment and inflation as well as the comparative economic status of two nations. It can even guide domestic fiscal and monetary policy. Companies also pick up on these details as they search out opportunities to cut costs or increase revenues by expanding their operations internationally.

Let's say our country is a very large net importer but also has high unemployment. This situation could indicate that the foreign nations exporting goods to us have an advantage over us in the production of those goods—for example, their labor costs may be less than ours. If that's the case, and you work in an industry that produces goods that are being imported in large numbers, look for downward pressure on your wages.

21. CAPITAL ACCOUNT

The capital account is the other half of the majority of exchanges that take place in the balance of payments. Anytime a store buys or sells a product, it's not just the product or service itself that changes hands; there's also a change in an agreed-upon value of capital ownership. Remember our example of the bottle of gin selling for $35—the storekeeper gives you the bottle of gin (increasing the value of goods in your possession), and you give him $35 (increasing the amount of capital in his possession).

This same basic system is true for trade between nations. When a nation exports something, in return they receive currency, or some other form of capital compensation, for the goods. Anytime a nation increases its ownership of capital from another nation, that's included on the capital account. If that same nation decreases its capital, giving it to another nation, then that decreases the value of its own capital account. The capital account, in other words, measures changes in capital ownership.

These changes can include money earned and spent from the export and import of products and services (those things found in the current account). But the capital account also measures investments in other nations through the purchase of companies, opening branches of companies, or investing in the stocks and bonds of that nation. A decrease in the capital account is almost always associated with an increase in the current account and vice versa since a nation doesn't give away capital without receiving something in return. Often such an increase is in the form of cash, but it might also come in the form of development, such as the construction of a factory.

What You Should Know

The capital account is a summary of the investments that occur between nations. It includes foreign direct investments (which occur when a company opens a branch or subsidiary in a foreign nation, either alone or as part of some level of partnership or joint venture), purchases and sales of stocks and bonds, and land ownership. Anything that alters the ownership stake in a nation's economic future across international boundaries is included in the capital account.

Cash, in itself, is a form of investment in another nation. When Nation A gives Nation B goods in exchange for Nation B's currency, that currency is accepted because Nation A is confident that it will be able to use that currency at some point in the future to receive an amount of goods equal to or greater in value than the amount of goods it gave to obtain that currency. This is why the people of one nation have reason to wish the economy of another nation well—they want to receive some positive return on their investment.

The information derived from the capital account gives a couple of interesting pieces of information about a nation's currency, its growth, its international interdependence, and its overall ability to attract investments. For example, if we know that Nation A has a very high capital account surplus but a high exchange rate relative to an export partner, Nation B, we might predict that Nation A's currency will decrease in value relative to Nation B, since demand for that currency will decrease along with the lower demand for Nation A's goods.

Why You Should Care

Despite being at least as important as the current account, if not more so, the capital account gets very little public attention. As a result, there is a lot of misconception about the very nature of trade itself; people look only at the current account and forget about the related investments that occur.

You should care about the capital account because it fills in the second half of the balance of payments, providing the full picture of a nation's international transactions. This alone gives you a better understanding of how trade influences your nation.

The information derived from the capital account also provides a view of the flow of investments that a nation is experiencing, allowing people to project future cross-national investment patterns. This is particularly important for investors, but it also allows companies to consider means of raising capital, or to help individuals project changes in exchange rates.

As with using other portions of the balance of payments for economic projections, it's important to remember that this is only one small piece of the picture, a single landmark on a long road trip. Still, when it comes to money people don't like to screw around, so use all the tools available to you, particularly when it comes to domestic policy that influences your ability to earn a living.

22. TRANSFER PAYMENTS

The final portion of the balance of payments is often referred to as the balancing account. This is the portion that accounts for unilateral transfers between nations. Some transactions occur in which something of value is given without any reciprocation; this is called a transfer payment. Since the balance of payments, as a whole, must balance, any transactions of this type will have an impact on either the capital or current accounts, *but not both*. The balancing value that makes the entire balance of payments equivalent is included in the transfer payments portion of the balance of payments.

- If a transaction that affects the transfer payments account influenced the current account, it means that the nation either gave or received goods and/or services without expectations of providing something of equal value in return.
- If a transaction that affects the transfer payments account influenced the capital account, then the nation either gave or received capital ownership or some form of investment ownership without doing anything to earn that ownership.

What You Should Know

Only a very narrow set of transactions fall within the transfer payments. Still, despite being very limited in scope, they occur frequently around the world. Emergency assistance is probably the clearest example of such a transaction. The aid the United States sent to Haiti after the 2010 earthquake was a form of transfer payment. The United States shipped food, clean water, and medical supplies to the stricken nation without expectation of receiving any payment. Such a transaction had an impact on the values of both the current account and the transfer payments account, but since the United States received no ownership rights to capital in exchange for those goods, the transaction did not influence the capital account at all.

Similar transactions that influence the transfer payments account could include the movement of capital between nations that aren't for transactions reasons. For example, if Canada were to provide Switzerland with the rights to a bit of land in order to build an embassy, this would fall within transfer payments. In the case of a private company, this sort of transaction might take the form of a transfer of funds between the parent company and a foreign subsidiary.

Why You Should Care

This account may challenge what you think you know about the trade of your nation. Although information about transfer payments isn't very useful by itself, given that it doesn't have any direct application to normal trade, it *does* play a role in your nation's balance of payments as a whole.

23. TRADE IMBALANCE

When people talk about trade imbalances, they are really referring to either a positive or negative value in the current account. A trade surplus occurs when a nation exports more goods than it imports. As of this writing, China has the world's largest trade surplus because the rest of the world purchases far more Chinese goods and services than China buys from the rest of the world.

In the opposite direction, a trade deficit occurs when a nation imports more goods than it exports. The United States currently has the world's largest trade deficit because it purchases far more goods and services from other nations than it exports. The vast majority of trade transactions, however, are balanced.

What You Should Know

The very term "trade imbalance" is misleading, as it implies that in trading, one nation benefits at the expense of another. Except for transfer payments, which typically represent an insignificant proportion of a nation's total trade, in the long run *the value exchanged between nations is equal.* (At least an exchange of value is so close to equivalent that the only people really concerned with the difference are professional economists.)

You may find this concept a bit strange. After all, isn't international trade like our own spending habits, writ large? If a nation is maintaining a trade deficit, then isn't it spending too much money on imports?

Well, no.

The thing that truly matters is not whether your nation has a trade deficit or not, but *what that trade deficit is funding.* Don't think of importing goods and services in terms of consumer spending; instead, it's like capital investment using a very big coupon.

For instance, Nation A takes advantage of the lower costs and higher volume of goods obtained by importing from Nation B, which has an advantage in a particular set of goods and services. Nation A then uses those imports (which created a trade deficit) to create other goods and services of value; in other words, Nation A improves its return on investment.

If a company purchases a machine from some other company, we could say they're giving money to the other company rather than keeping it. But in the long run they have increased their production efficiency and future production potential. They've concentrated on what they're good at. This allows them to attract buyers of their products. In the same way in our example above, Nation B uses its reserves of the foreign currency it had previously received from Nation A to purchase that nation's exports.

(Remember what I said before: In the long run, international trade is a zero-sum game.)

Although a trade surplus is the opposite of a trade deficit, the goal is basically the same: earn a return on investment. Rather than investing in its own economy using capital from other nations, a nation running a trade surplus is attempting to invest in another nation's economy using its own capital.

Would you exchange your goods or services to someone who tried to pay you with fake money? Of course not, because it's worthless and you couldn't use it for anything—unless the person paying you accepted the same money in return for their own goods and services. The same can be said for nations. When Nation A exports goods to Nation B, it receives currency or some other form of ownership interest in the future production potential of Nation B. Nation A believes this currency will purchase an equal or greater amount of goods from either Nation B or some other nation that intends to purchase goods and services from Nation B. Either way, the money that a nation with a trade deficit spends will eventually come back to it.

In the case of the United States and China, China currently holds one of the largest reserves of U.S. dollars in the world. China has also been struggling to manage price inflation, while in the aftermath of the 2007 financial collapse the United States has been experiencing price decreases associated with a struggling economy. As prices between the two nations begin to balance out, those currency reserves will eventually come back to the United States. Individuals and organizations in China will find it cheaper to purchase an increasing number of goods and services from the United States rather than to purchase them domestically. The trade imbalance between these two nations will continue to decrease over time as each nation focuses on producing a narrower set of goods and services within their respective comparative advantages.

Why You Should Care

A country can sustain a deficit as long as other nations see it as a suitable investment. A country can run a trade surplus so long as it is able to generate enough demand that people are willing to trade capital (such as money) to purchase the nation's goods and services. The real thing we should concern ourselves with is exactly what the people and organizations of other nations are interested in and whether our country is able to take advantage of the opportunities available.

A nation can create a trade deficit in order to purchase the supplies necessary to improve its own production potential and produce goods in value far greater than it will have to sell when other nations purchase goods from it. This will create net value using comparative advantage. A nation can create a trade surplus in order to acquire ownership in one or more nations that it hopes will increase in value through improved production potential, exchange rate, and returns on investment.

24. FACTOR PRICE EQUALIZATION

Two nations that are economically integrated (meaning their governments have eliminated many barriers to trade and work to facilitate trade between nations) and that have a significant amount of trade between them will experience something called factor price equalization. Put simply, this means that the longer they trade freely with each other, the more pricing differentials between them will decrease.

This is a direct outgrowth of trade. If two nations can produce a good of comparable quality (say, an automobile), but one is cheaper than another, clearly the people of both nations will want to purchase the cheaper automobile. This forces the companies in the more expensive nation to either lower prices or go out of business. The other nation's companies can increase their prices to meet the production demands of orders for new automobiles.

Let's expand that scenario beyond trade in a single good. Now that some people have lost their jobs in Nation A because Nation B's cars are more competitive, the workers of Nation A decrease their own spending because of their lower income—they've got less so they spend less. They must find new work in a sector in which their nation is more competitive on an international level (say, computers). Either way, prices for automobiles will come down in Nation A, either because companies are using fewer workers to produce an equal amount of goods, or because they're simply producing fewer goods.

In Nation B, orders for automobiles are up. Because of that, following the law of supply and demand, car prices will start to increase. In Nation A, the same thing is happening with computer prices—they're rising to meet increased demand, while in Nation B (which isn't as good at producing computers as it is at making cars), the price of computers is sinking in order to stay competitive.

Once pricing between the two nations reaches equilibrium (in other words, they're both producing goods at nearly equal average price levels, trading only in those goods wherein each has a comparative advantage) then the price increases and decreases resulting from factor price equalization will effectively stop.

The above example is theoretical. With the arguable exception of North Korea, no nation in the world trades with only one other nation. Should either of the nations in the above example begin trading with another nation, Nation C, that has lower prices than either of them for either cars or computers, they will experience additional benefits as they acquire more goods at much lower prices, improving efficiency in national resource usage, decreasing costs and prices of their own production, and so forth. It can become very complicated very quickly, but only due to the large volume of trade between many different nations; the same basic principles hold consistent.

What You Should Know

Factor price equalization occurs as a result of competition. A bag of rice, regardless of where it's produced in the world, will require the same factors of production: land, water, fertilizer, seeds, labor, and whatever else goes into growing rice. These factors, sometimes designated as raw materials and labor, are a primary determinant in the price levels of a particular nation. As access to the resources in each nation becomes increasingly available to those of other nations through increased globalization, the costs of the factors of production tend to equalize, causing average price levels in each nation to resemble each other by either increasing or decreasing. The general takeaway here, then, is that *in the long run international trade benefits you, the consumer.*

Factor price equalization, when first established as an economic theory in the early twentieth century, referred only to nations that were next to each other, or at least near enough to each other so they had equal access to the factors of production. In the modern era, however, as globalization increases and nations increase the volume of trade and degree of economic integration, this principle is influencing trade relations between even very geographically disparate nations.

Why You Should Care

In projecting how future trade will change between nations, factor price equalization plays an important role. As each company attempts to lower its own costs, it will eventually acquire resources either directly or indirectly from a foreign nation with the lowest prices. With a bit of industry knowledge and some economic savvy, it's possible to estimate changes in costs and pricing strategies.

If two companies produce different goods, each in a different nation, and one nation has significantly lower average price levels, the company that works in the nation with the higher price levels can expect its goods to become more competitive in the nation with lower price levels. The ability to predict such movements in import and export levels as a result of price changes is important in understanding what to expect from your company's future competitiveness on an international scale.

25. MERCANTILISM

For centuries, the dominant economic theory was mercantilism. It was particularly influential in the seventeenth and eighteenth centuries until it was undermined by Adam Smith in his book *The Wealth of Nations.*

Mercantilism argues that the factors of production are fixed and that for a nation to increase in wealth, it must do so at the cost of other nations' wealth. Mercantilists believed that a nation must maintain a trade surplus in order to accumulate wealth, and that any trade deficit depletes the nation's total wealth. Money was representative only of the amount of raw minerals, usually gold and silver, a nation possessed. In other words, a nation only had as much wealth as the volume of precious metals it kept in its possession.

Since gold, silver, and the currency based solely on them were the preferred methods of paying for goods in the seventeenth and eighteenth centuries, even through trade, it stands to reason that those nations running trade deficits would deplete their resources. This was particularly the case since much of the period was marked by wars that were often waged by mercenary troops, who were paid using the national reserves of gold and silver. As a result, the coffers of many nations were quite frequently empty.

The logic of this economic philosophy drove nations in wars waged simply to obtain another country's assets; it also frequently resulted in rebellions by the mercenaries when the government was unwilling or unable to pay them.

What You Should Know

Today we can see the weaknesses of mercantilist theory, as expressed by figures such as Jean-Baptiste Colbert (1619–1683), Louis XIV's minister of finance. The belief that any trade deficit depletes a nation's wealth kept some nations from experiencing the full gains to be realized from trade. National policies that maintained the gold and silver supplies required to back up any currency (or to have available currency at all) required nations to avoid exporting these precious metals. As a result, nations frequently did not take advantage of cheaper or better foreign goods. Trade occurred on a more limited scale. Under a mercantilist philosophy, it also becomes exceedingly difficult to align domestic economic policy that best benefits one's country with the international needs associated with that nation's trade as well as the management of its currency.

Why You Should Care

Somewhat surprisingly, mercantilism, or at least remnants of it, has survived into the modern era. A small but very vocal population calls for a metal-centric economic policy to be reinstated, despite its obvious shortcomings.

It's not as if we've not tried this stuff before. The gold standard, for instance, was a system by which currency was freely and readily exchanged for a fixed amount of gold (discussed more in Chapter 4), requiring a nation to maintain minimum levels of gold. This system is once again growing in popularity among economics undergraduate students and some fringe economists and politicians. The reality, though, is that, as with all forms of mercantilism, it is impossible to maintain in the twenty-first century just as was the case in the eighteenth, nineteenth, and twentieth centuries and before for the very same reasons: *Mercantilism has an adverse effect on trade, which modern economies cannot afford.*

The United States formally went off the gold standard in 1971 during the Nixon administration and it seems unlikely to come back. While mercantilism shouldn't affect you directly—assuming that people have enough sense to avoid implementing such a system again—it's extremely important to be aware of how it works.

CHAPTER 4

Currency

Despite being labeled as one of the most villainous and malignant ideas ever devised, money plays a very important role in the lives of most people. Even those who hate it probably wouldn't freely dispense with their own savings and income.

The reality is a bit less dramatic. Money is just a method for keeping track of debts owed for goods and services.

After all, if it couldn't be exchanged for goods or services, money would just be little bits of paper and metal with no practical function. Adam Smith, often considered to be the founder of modern economics, noted the paradox of value: Water is among the most useful of all resources yet gold, which is far less useful, is considered to be of higher value. It's precisely *because* currency has little or no intrinsic value that it can be used exclusively as an intermediary of exchange.

How exactly does this work? Let's imagine that two people (call them Sam and Janet) want to exchange goods or services. Sam has nothing Janet wants, but she has something Sam wants. Alternately, Sam wants something of Janet's, but he doesn't intend to receive all or part of his share of the exchange immediately. What Sam and Janet both need is a method of tracking the value of these exchanges.

To make this a bit more concrete: Sam wants $10 worth of bread from Janet, the baker. He offers her, in return, $10 worth of whatever service he has on hand (say, mowing lawns). Janet doesn't want her lawn mown, though. So, instead of mowing her lawn, Sam gives Janet $10 worth of money. Janet can use the $10 in money to purchase something else from Ralph. Ralph now owns that $10 worth of money. He comes back to Sam with the expectation that Sam will fulfill his obligation for the purchase of bread by mowing Ralph's lawn, even though Ralph has given Sam nothing (except the money). In a similar manner, perhaps Janet wants her lawn mown, but not right away. She and Sam use the $10 as a method of tracking the debt Sam owes Janet—at some point in the future, he'll mow her lawn.

These are the original roots of currency. It's nothing more than an "I owe you" letter for goods and services. The underlying resources are what give currency its value, not some belief that money itself has an inherent value separate from what it can be used to redeem.

What makes money so important is the fact that nearly all people in the world recognize what it represents and are willing to exchange things of actual usefulness for it. This is a key point, which is why I keep coming back to it: *Money in and of itself is worthless. Its value comes from what it represents.*

In the international arena, not all currencies are recognized as having the same value. It's central to keeping international trade flowing smoothly that people agree upon how much different types of currency are worth, both as a measure of underlying goods and services and as a way in which currencies can be exchanged for each other. This is determined by a number of factors, including the basic supply and demand for a currency, the underlying value of the goods and services that a currency's nation produces, and domestic economic policy.

While the underlying nature of currency has not changed since its original inception, it's now far more sophisticated. In the modern era there are many types of currency, with differences ranging from the amount of goods that can be purchased per unit to how much of one currency can be purchased with another. The valuations, exchanges, and methods of managing currency have all become very involved but not at all difficult to understand. Learning how currency works will very much improve your ability to manage your money. Particularly in the international environment, which includes some additional complexities that provide the opportunity to benefit or the risk of harm, your financial security depends on how well you understand the nature of currency transactions.

26. FIXED EXCHANGE RATES

An exchange rate is how much of one currency you can buy with another. For example, at the time of this writing, one U.S. dollar will buy exactly 0.7641 euros (which would be written as USD1 = EUR0.7641). The inverse value is EUR1 = USD1.3087. One unit of a particular currency will purchase a number of units (or a fraction of a unit) of some other currency.

There are two primary types of exchange rates. The easiest of these to understand is the fixed exchange rate, also called a pegged exchange rate. A fixed exchange rate is one in which the value of one currency is exchanged at exactly the same rate as another currency, no matter how this other currency fluctuates. For instance, if the Mexican peso is fixed to the U.S. dollar at a one-to-one rate (where MXN1 = USD1), then no matter how the U.S. dollar changes value compared to any other currency in the world, the exchange rate between the dollar and the peso will remain the same. The implication of this is that if the exchange rate of the U.S. dollar to the British pound goes up 10 percent, then the exchange rate between the Mexican peso and the British pound will also go up by 10 percent because of the rate fix between the dollar and the peso.

For a currency to adopt a fixed-exchange rate-to-change value (that is, for the value at which the exchange rate is fixed to change) there must be a change in official government policy. This happens quite commonly among fixed currencies.

What You Should Know

A nation typically chooses to fix its exchange rate in order to stabilize exchange rate fluctuations. Nations with smaller economies often have trouble managing volatility in the value of their exchange rate relative to other nations, creating uncertainty that causes big problems in trade. Rather than risk economic troubles that could destabilize the entire nation's political and social infrastructure, the leaders of such a nation will usually opt, instead, to just peg their exchange rate to a currency that is more stable. This is particularly the case with nations that either rely on goods that have seasonal production cycles or have economies that lack diversification.

Exchange rates are rarely fixed to just a single currency. Usually a fixed exchange rate is set at a value that is an average of several different currencies, called a "basket." These currencies are chosen from either the nation's largest trading partners or those economically larger nations that are geographically nearby.

A country can also choose to peg its currency to commonly traded commodities such as gold and platinum or it can use such precious metals as an element in its currency basket. In 2005, for example, China's currency (the renminbi, RMB) was pegged at a value that combines the average of ten different currencies. However, some of the currencies in this basket are worth more in the average than others. This is accomplished by using what is called a weighted average. Rather than adding up all the values then dividing by the number of currencies used, as in a normal average, a weighted average multiplies each value by the percentage of the total that the value represents.

Why You Should Care

Many nations around the world have fixed currencies; some of them, such as China, are very large economic players. When an American company buys something from these nations or sells something to them, it matters whether the product or service is listed in the domestic or foreign currency. Any time that capital crosses international boundaries, either by way of a purchase, investment, or transfer, there is a very good chance that one of the nations involved has a fixed currency and an even better chance that somewhere along the supply chain a nation with a fixed currency contributed to the value of the transfer in an indirect manner. Since the rate at which these nations fix their currencies to another currency influences how expensive their goods are to other nations, you must pay careful attention to the peg that these nations choose.

The exchange rate is also important if you're planning any international travel. If you know the exchange rate between the United States and Europe is something on the order of USD1 = EUR2, this might be a good time to take that vacation to France you've been planning. After all, one of your American dollars will buy two euros worth of French wine and chocolate!

The peg that a nation with a fixed exchange rate chooses doesn't change the price of that nation's goods in its own currency—not directly anyway, since something that sells at RMB100 will always still sell at RMB100, whether China's peg to the U.S. dollar is set at 100 percent (a one-to-one ratio) or 1,000 percent (a ten-to-one ratio). However, for those outside of China, the rate at which the RMB is pegged to the dollar will determine how much of their own currency they have to spend to acquire each RMB, which makes the currency itself more or less expensive. The result for China's exports to the rest of the world, then, is that the exports themselves become more or less expensive depending on which currencies are used to purchase them. At the same time, foreign goods will also be more or less expensive as the Chinese purchase other currencies using the RMB.

Why should you care about nations with fixed currencies? Because more likely than not you've bought goods or services from a nation that has a fixed currency, and the rate at which they fix that currency will have an influence on your own finances.

27. DEVALUATION AND REVALUATION

Just because a nation has a fixed exchange rate doesn't mean that its exchange rate can't be changed. The process by which a fixed currency changes value by itself, without the value of the currency to which it is pegged changing in equal proportion, is very simple but can either strengthen the country's economy or bring about a regionalized economic apocalypse.

A fixed exchange rate changes value when the government of that nation decides to change the value at which the currency is fixed. Let's say the U.S. dollar and Mexican peso are exchanged at a one-to-one ratio (USD1 = MXN1) because the Mexican peso is pegged to the U.S. dollar. The Mexican government wants to decrease the exchange rate of its currency; they issue a statement that one dollar now equals, for example, 0.75 pesos. Such a change is called *devaluation*—the Mexican government, which has a fixed currency, has lowered its exchange rate. The U.S. dollar now buys fewer pesos.

The opposite move, wherein a fixed currency increases its exchange rate, is called *revaluation*. Using the same basic example as before (which was chosen for its simplicity rather than any sort of accuracy regarding the exchange rate or currency policy of the nations discussed), should the Mexican government decide that they want to revalue the peg on their currency by 25 percent, from USD1 = MXN1, then the new exchange rate would be set to USD1 = MXN1.25, using Mexican federal economic policy as the mechanism for the change.

What You Should Know

The ability to manage the rate at which a fixed currency is exchanged is critical to maintaining economic stability. Nations will periodically alter their exchange rate in order to account for any changes to their economic growth. If a nation's domestic prices go up or down significantly as a result of its level of growth and inflation, but the country's exchange rate does not change, that will cause imports and exports to be either artificially high or low.

- If prices go up, the country's imports will rise (because people are buying cheaper foreign goods) and its exports will fall (because people in other countries don't want to buy more expensive goods).
- If prices go down, the country's imports will fall (because no one wants to buy foreign goods that are more expensive than domestic ones) and exports will increase (because it costs people in other countries less money to buy them than it does to buy goods made in their own countries).

The important thing to remember here is what happens when a nation revalues or devalues its currency, and what the influence will be on international capital movement. It is not a difficult thing to learn, but there are cases throughout history of nations severely misunderstanding the implications of fixed exchange rate management.

In 1991, Argentina pegged its currency to the U.S. dollar at a one-to-one ratio; however, its inflation rate was much higher than that of the United States during the same period. Even though the Argentine peso was able to purchase far, far less than the dollar, the exchange rate between the two was equal. The result was that Argentina had some of the most expensive exports in all the Americas, making them extremely uncompetitive in the international marketplace. The other consequence was that imports from other nations were cheaper than domestic Argentine goods, so imports increased as well. The lack of demand for Argentine goods caused inflation to steadily grow for over a decade until its peak of 17.3 percent in 2003. What brought down unemployment and saved the economy from total devastation? A number of things, but one of the most important was a 2002 policy that devalued the Argentine peso from ARS1 = USD1 to ARS1.4 = USD1, then allowed the ARS to float. Within two months of removing the peg entirely and allowing the peso to float (floating currencies are discussed in the next topic), the ARS was exchanging at ARS3.5 = USD1. Argentine exports fell in price and were now in demand, and unemployment rates consistently dropped again to still high but now manageable levels.

Why You Should Care

One of the most difficult predictions in international economics is fluctuations in exchange rates. For companies that have foreign branches or those that do extensive amounts of trade, such fluctuations in exchange rates can become either extremely expensive or extremely beneficial. These companies do all they can to predict these exchange rate fluctuations and manage how they react to them. This also affects you, the consumer.

You live in Thailand and plan to purchase a pumped-up Ferrari for exactly 1 million euros (just go with it; it's an example). At the time you sign the contract, that equals 40 million Thai baht, but one month later when you go to exchange your baht for euros, the Thai government decided to change its pegged exchange and now 1 million euros is equal to 50 million baht. No Ferrari for you!

Even though fluctuations this large are not very common, they do happen from time to time, and smaller fluctuations happen quite frequently. The influence that such a change in exchange rate has on the price of imports and exports can also cause prices across the nation to increase. If the price of a nation's imports increases as a result of devaluation, then the companies that import those goods and services will have to charge higher prices to make up for the higher cost of production.

28. FLOATING EXCHANGE RATES

The exchange rates of a floating currency are determined in a slightly different manner than those of fixed currency. Instead of being set by a government agency at a fixed rate of exchange with some other currency, a floating exchange rate is set by both the people selling the currency and those buying the same currency. These market forces of supply and demand are considered to be the primary determinants of the rates by which floating currencies exchange. That being said, the supply and demand for a floating currency can each be altered using domestic fiscal policy (the policies that control taxation and government spending) and fiscal policy (the policies that control the quantity of the money supply and interest rates, the latter of which are considered to be the price of money).

Given that every nation with a floating currency influences its currency's exchange rate, the idea of a fully floating currency is little more than theory. The reality is that the closest most nations come to a pure float is something called a managed float, wherein the nation allows its exchange rates to be controlled by supply and demand, but the government takes steps to influence supply and demand for its currency.

Foreign currency transactions for floating currencies happen in a manner quite similar to that by which investors perform trades in stock. There's an asking price, which is the price at which someone is willing to sell a certain amount of currency for another. For instance, suppose the cheapest someone is willing to sell 100 British pounds (GBP100) in exchange for Canadian dollars is CAD200, in which case the asking price of GBP1 is CAD2. There is also a bidding price, which is the highest amount that someone is willing to purchase a currency for in terms of another currency. Let's say someone is willing to pay CAD150 for GBP100. That would mean the bid value for GBP1 is CAD1.5. The difference between the ask and the bid prices is called the spread. In this example, the spread is CAD0.5, since the ask is CAD2.0 and the bid is CAD1.5. In order for the transaction to take place, either the buyer or the seller must compromise on the price. Transactions quite frequently occur through an intermediary that makes its profit off the spread.

Such exchanges typically take place electronically in large quantities, but smaller quantities that aren't significant enough to influence exchange rates happen quite frequently as well. Next time you're in the international terminal of your favorite airport, take a close look around and you'll find a booth for exchanging currency. Usually it'll have the spot rates listed on an electronic billboard (the spot rate is the exchange rate by which you can exchange currency immediately in a single transaction; this is opposed to some other forms of transactions that include future transfers of money). You walk up, give them your currency, and tell them which currency you want in exchange. They make their money by taking advantage of the spread, offering only the ask price for each currency because they know people will pay it for the small denominations of currency being exchanged. Banks will sometimes do this as well, although it can be difficult to find some of the more obscure international currencies except in large denomination orders.

What You Should Know

Despite the seeming simplicity of what amounts to an auction system for foreign exchange transactions, the complexity of these floating exchange rates is amplified when you consider the multitude of influences that determine currency prices. Changes to a number of indirect factors cause not only valid changes in the valuation but also speculative changes made by investors. These in turn make variations in foreign exchange rates among floating currencies extremely common and, at times, extremely fast. The saving grace is that, as noted, floating currencies also tend to be associated with extremely stable economies, so that the changes that occur in the rate between two floating currencies will be so small that they only amount to a significant value for those organizations exchanging in very large quantities.

The primary determinant of the value of a nation's floating currency is the value of that nation's underlying production. The total value of a nation's economy, as measured by the value of its production (usually using GDP, discussed in Chapter 10), is represented by the nation's money, and if that number changes, the value of a floating currency in the foreign exchange market also changes. As people invest in that nation's economy by trading their own national resources for a share of the nation's currency, they are investing in that nation's future production potential under the belief that the nation will produce enough to give the currency value as a form of exchange for more goods and services at a later date.

There are a great number of other factors involved in determining floating exchange rates. To summarize, you're watching for any economic changes that will influence the amount of currency that the people of a particular nation might want. You can expect anything that would increase exports to some nation to have an influence on decreasing the exchange rate for that nation's currency as your own currency increases in value.

Why You Should Care

Most of the world's economically largest nations use floating currencies, and the majority of currencies in the world that are considered to be reserve currencies (those currencies that are held on reserve in large quantities by foreign nations for use as a very commonly accepted or demanded currency for global use) are floating currencies. If you've ever engaged in any sort of international trade, there is a strong likelihood that you've done trade with a nation that maintains a floating exchange rate.

As noted, exchange rates among floating currencies normally vary only to a very small degree at any given point in time, typically measured to hundredths of a percent, called pips (percentage in points). That's not to say that the rate changes are too small to influence individuals, however. If a company experiences a cost increase associated with higher exchange rates, that cost increase will often translate into higher prices for people purchasing its products. The reverse can be said for lower exchange rates, though. It pays to watch floating rates carefully and see how changes are reflected in consumer prices.

29. DEPRECIATION AND APPRECIATION

Rather than being changed by governmental directive, the change in a floating exchange rate is determined by the manner in which buyers and sellers determine the current and estimated future values of the currency. Since this is different from the manner in which fixed exchange rates are altered, the changes in the value of a floating currency are given a unique label. When a floating currency decreases in value relative to another currency, this is called depreciation. When a floating currency increases in value, requiring more of a foreign currency to purchase an equal quantity of the domestic currency, it's called appreciation. Note that all calculations of exchange rate reflect a comparison of only two types of currency. So while a floating currency might appreciate against one currency, it could simultaneously depreciate against a different currency.

For example, we can imagine the currency of Nation A appreciating against the currency of Nation B as a result of Nation B experiencing high levels of inflation caused by reckless economic policies. At the same time, Currency A depreciates against Currency C as exports from Nation C increase, forcing many in Nation A to demand greater volume of Currency C.

Seen from the point of view of Nation B, its currency is depreciating against both currencies A and C due to lower trade volume and high inflation resulting from a tax on imports. Currency C, meanwhile, appreciates against both currencies A and B because of higher demand for Nation C's exports. The reason for the increased demand: The prices of Nation C's nearest competitor, Nation B, have recently increased dramatically as a result of tariffs imposed by C's government.

As the above example shows, floating exchange rates do not change in absolute terms, only in relative terms—relative to the value of other currencies, the same as fixed exchange rates. Unlike fixed exchange rates, however, you only need to evaluate the economic and trade conditions of the two nations in question.

What You Should Know

What types of things, exactly, influence the floating exchange rate, then? There are a number of internal and external factors. The most important determinant is the value of the nation's production that underlies the currency. After all, the value of a floating currency is only maintained by the nation's ability to produce goods and services for which the currency can be exchanged. As a nation produces a greater value of goods and services for the quantity of currency produced, the currency will be worth more, given its relative ability to purchase more for an equal quantity of currency. This ties in closely with national inflation, discussed in more detail in topic 32.

In addition, some of the following factors can influence the floating exchange rate:

- Higher inflation will push down exchange rates temporarily since the current quantity of currency held can purchase fewer goods.
- Any domestic fiscal or monetary policy that alters inflation and growth levels within the nation will have an influence on floating exchange rates.
- Speculative investors who believe that the currency will either increase or decrease relative to another currency can, at times, force large enough transactions to alter an exchange rate.
- Political issues can influence floating exchange rates. OPEC's threat to stop using the U.S. dollar as a reserve currency caused many speculators to panic and sell their dollars, pushing down the value of the dollar relative to the euro.

Floating exchange rates can also become either undervalued or overvalued. Not only do people often not have perfect information, but often having the proper information doesn't always matter. Whether people are investing and exchanging based on imperfect data or changes to the economic conditions, the reality is that floating exchange rates are in a constant state of flux that doesn't always represent the true value of the exchange.

Often, speculative investors will attempt to find these deviations in the price and value of a currency and invest accordingly so as to increase their own income. This process is called arbitrage. At other times, particularly for businesses whose primary operation is not financial in nature, the best option is to simply avoid the risk as much as possible.

Why You Should Care

Regardless of whether the new exchange rate following a fluctuation is a fair rate or not, the very nature of the rate changing allows for both opportunities and threats for those individuals and organizations that make foreign currency transactions even irregularly. Depending on how savvy you are in foreign exchange transactions as well as any transactions that involve foreign exchange (i.e., imports/exports, capital movement between parent and subsidiary, etc.), you can generate significant earnings based purely on variations in foreign exchange rates.

30. PURCHASING POWER PARITY

Maybe you've heard someone mention how cheap the cost of living is in another country, or that prices are a lot higher in some other place halfway around the world. That's because not every currency has the same purchasing power.

If, using only one unit of your own currency you can purchase ten units of some other currency, but prices in that foreign nation are also exactly ten times higher than in your native land, you will use exactly the same number of units of your own currency to purchase foreign goods. Sound confusing? Let's use a quick example.

Japanese Beer: JPY1,000
Indian Beer: INR100
Exchange Rate: INR1 = JPY10

We can see that someone from India could use 100 Indian rupees in order to purchase beer in their own nation. Or he or she could exchange the same number of rupees to get enough Japanese yen to purchase beer in Japan—because beer in Japan costs ten times what it costs in India.

Purchasing power means the ability of a currency to be exchanged for goods. Perhaps something you can buy for four dollars in the United States costs 320 yen in Japan. To the Japanese, 320 yen may not seem any more expensive than four dollars to someone from the United States, since the Japanese also make more yen at work than people from the United States make in dollars. All this means is that one yen doesn't have the same amount of purchasing power as the dollar, so it takes a lot more yen to purchase something than dollars. However, it's not uncommon to walk around carrying several thousand yen since that composes only a small proportion of what the average person makes (in the same way that four dollars is a very small proportion of what the average American makes).

We can apply the principles of purchasing power to even different parts of the same nation—the average income in New

York City is a lot higher than the average income in Omaha, Nebraska, but the prices in Omaha are also a lot lower, so every person is spending less money to maintain a lifestyle that's equal to or better than that of New York (although New Yorkers would probably strongly dispute that). That's because the purchasing power of the dollar varies across geographic locations.

Whereas purchasing power measures the ability of a currency to purchase goods, a more useful measure for determining the value of a currency on an international level is purchasing power parity. Purchasing power parity (PPP) is the ability of one nation's currency to purchase goods in a different nation. In other words, this compares how different currencies function in the same country, rather than trying to compare different currencies in different countries. It's expressed as follows:

PPP = Foreign Price using Foreign Currency/Domestic Price using Domestic Currency

How does this work in practice? Say, PPP = AUD4.56/USD4.07 = 1.12. So, the PPP between the Australian dollar and the U.S. dollar is AUD1.12 per USD1.

In other words, the U.S. dollar purchases slightly more than the Australian dollar—about 12 percent. The AUD has a PPP of 1.12, since it takes 1.12 AUD for every USD to purchase the same goods.

What You Should Know

The difference between the exchange rate of the currency and the ability of that currency to purchase goods makes it seem as if the goods of one nation are relatively more expensive or cheaper for people of other nations. If the currency's exchange rate is significantly greater than the currency's PPP, then the currency is overvalued. This makes that nation's exports appear more expensive since you have to use more of your own currency to purchase enough foreign currency to buy whatever it is you're trying to import. The flip side to this is that when a currency's exchange rate is significantly lower than its PPP, it is undervalued. This causes that nation's exports to appear cheaper to foreigners since they have to exchange less of their own currency to purchase those goods. Let's take a look at an example:

Cost of a burger in the United States: USD4.07
Cost of a burger in Japan: JPY320
Exchange rate: JPY78.4 = USD1

Using the information above, we can figure out the PPP between the United States and Japan. Start with the cost of a burger in the United States—we pay $4.07. Now exchange that value at the current exchange rate, and you get JPY319. Uh-oh! You don't have enough Japanese yen to purchase a burger in Japan because the exchange rate is different than the PPP rate. In this case, Japan's currency is overvalued compared to the dollar because equivalent goods cannot be purchased in Japan using the current exchange rate.

Another way to look at it is that the U.S. dollar is undervalued compared to the yen; remember that exchange rates are all relative between two currencies. (In these metrics the larger or more prominent currency is normally compared against the lesser currency. However, we could make an exception if there is some reason to believe that the larger currency is artificially high or low in value compared to another.)

A very popular index for measuring PPP and whether a currency is over- or undervalued, titled the Big Mac Index, was developed by *The Economist* magazine. Meant to be a bit humorous, the Big Mac Index lists the price of a Big Mac from McDonald's restaurants in each nation. Although it's usually recommended that you use several different types of prices to determine average price differences between nations, the Big Mac Index uses just the one, the price of a Big Mac, to determine the purchasing power parity for each nation. If the difference in price of a Big Mac between two nations, each nation using its respective currency, is not fully accounted for by the exchange rate between the two countries, then that currency is considered to be overvalued or undervalued.

Why You Should Care

The purchasing power parity between two nations is often considered to be a guideline for the exchange rate between the same nations. There are a number of cases throughout history where nations have been accused of keeping their exchange rate undervalued in order to make their exports cheaper. People tend to have very strong feelings about this, and some government policies are based on the belief that a single nation's currency is either over- or undervalued. People who complain about such currency manipulation are correct, in a sense, but are looking at far too short a timeframe.

Recall from Chapter 1 the idea of gains from trade. The people and organizations of each nation intentionally seek out other nations to purchase those resources that have lower prices. This often leads them to nations that have less developed economies. The lower costs of labor in these nations can result in significantly higher purchasing power parity for the foreign currency in that nation.

Does that mean that the leaders of the exporting nation are guilty of manipulating its exchange rate to intentionally undervalue its currency? They could be, but it's impossible to say based on just that information. It's equally impossible to assume that exchange rates will automatically and immediately adjust to ensure that average prices around the world are the same, as this would eliminate any opportunity a nation has to take advantage of an absolute advantage. Now recall from Chapter 3, in the section dealing with factor price equalization, that in the long term and with greater amounts of trade, prices in two nations will slowly change to more greatly resemble prices in the other.

Still, PPP plays an important role in estimating the value of a currency. Between two nations that are already relatively stable and have significant trade together, the deviation of exchange rate and PPP will be much smaller and adjustments will happen more immediately. Between nations that have little or no trade with one another, or for nations that have relatively less stable economies, these PPP-based over- and undervaluation estimates may do more to indicate the opportunity to take advantage of national trade advantages that may not adjust exchange rates for years or even decades.

In both cases, PPP is a useful tool for estimating movements between the exchange rates of nations. As with all things, the exact information you derive from PPP depends greatly on the context in which both nations are placed, but in all cases there is opportunity to either benefit from variations in exchange rate and/or variations in trade advantages.

31. INTEREST RATES

Monetary policy refers to two primary things:

1. Changes in the supply of money
2. Changes in the price of money

The former is relatively easy to understand: If the government prints more money or decreases the minimum requirements that banks must adhere to for the percentage of money they must keep in reserve, then the money supply increases. If the government increases the amount of money that banks must keep on hand (their reserve requirements) or prints less money than that which is destroyed during the normal activities of daily wear and tear, then the money supply decreases.

The price of money, though, is a little different. Isn't the price of everything else measured in money? How can money have a price? The answer is both simple and complex. It has to do with interest rates.

Whenever money is borrowed, it must be paid back with a little bit additional, called interest (Islamic banking handles interest in a slightly different manner but with the same end result). There are a number of different ways in which people and institutions borrow money. These include credit cards, various types of mortgages, consumer loans for things such as cars or furniture, and loans for individuals. There are also various types of business loans; for instance, bonds issued by companies or governments are a type of loan. Even the money you put into your savings account at the bank is borrowed by the bank and issued to people in the form of other types of loans. For the privilege of doing this, the bank pays you an interest rate (although it's lower than the interest rates they earn from issuing other loans; this is the primary way banks generate income). On top of all this, there are interest rates exclusive to loans between banks and other financial institutions.

There are far too many different individual interest rates to list here. While each can be individually controlled and has its own influence, which is important for more detailed analyses, our concern for the moment is an overall look at interest rates.

As interest rates increase, the amount of money that must be paid back for a loan also increases. As a result, economists say that when interest rates increase, the price of money goes up. Conversely, the price of money is said to have lowered when interest rates decrease. As you might guess, this impacts international trade and financing.

What You Should Know

Most of the time when people refer to interest rates, they are talking about the rates for federal treasury investments, both long and short term, as well as the rates charged on loans between banks. These are often called indicator rates, because these rates often influence a number of other interest rates and are a good indicator of how interest is going to be treated.

Now that we've narrowed down which interest rates to pay the most attention to, what the heck do you do with that information? The best thing you can do with it, if your interest is in global economics, is to compare rates between nations. In particular, there are two things to watch for: interest rate differentials between nations, and changes in those differentials.

When two nations have interest rates that differ from each other, the degree to which they differ is important. A nation that has higher interest rates than your own is a great place in which to invest, given the relatively high return you'll get (assuming exchange rates do not change in the meantime). On the other hand, it's poor for borrowing, since you'd have to pay back a greater amount than you would borrowing from a domestic institution. As a result, a differential in interest rates will cause the flow of international investments to shift, altering the amount of resources being allocated to economic growth in any particular nation.

In addition, a differential in interest rates will change the amount being borrowed in each nation. As a result, the amount of consumption and investments funded through lending will change in each nation, altering the amount of purchases, including exports and imports, between the two nations. Simply put, when two nations have interest rates that differ from one another, investments will go to the nation with the higher rate, while borrowing will come from the nation with the lower rate.

Why You Should Care

Something as simple as keeping track of a few indicator interest rates between two countries can very much contribute to the financial well-being of both the company you work for and, by extension, you. It's pretty easy to see the benefits associated with investing in nations at higher rates of return and borrowing from nations with lower interest rates. Although interest rates influence a number of other issues in global economics, these will be discussed in topic 33.

32. INFLATION RATES

We've talked about purchasing power already in topic 30. Purchasing power, you remember, is the ability of a currency to be exchanged for goods and services. The purchasing power of a currency can change; the rate at which it changes is called inflation. The term deflation is used to denote periods of negative inflation, a process by which purchasing power actually increases. This manifests itself as price and wage fluctuations. If, over the course of one or more years, overall average prices in a nation increase, that means you have to spend more money to purchase an equivalent amount of goods. This is inflation.

Of course, you may have received a wage increase, so while the price increase may force you to spend more money it is not necessarily costing you a higher percentage of your total income.

Still, each individual dollar can be exchanged for fewer goods, reducing the purchasing power of the currency. A trend in the opposite direction, in which each unit of a currency can purchase more goods, is called deflation. After 2007, the United States and much of Europe experienced a period of deflation during which prices for housing and a number of other goods decreased, allowing people to purchase a greater amount of goods for an equal amount of currency, or an equal amount of goods for less currency. This was generally good because many people lost their jobs forcing them to live on less income than they had previously done. (Note: Deflation is not always good. Steadily falling prices may indicate that an economy is in recession.)

Inflation is calculated as an average. Say, for instance, that the average price of goods and services in your nation goes up 100 percent over ten years. In that case, we would say that the average annual inflation rate in your nation has been 10 percent over the past ten years. During times of deflation, our inflation rate is negative. So if the average price of goods and services over a ten-year period decreases by 10 percent, we could say either that the nation has experienced a 1 percent annual deflation rate, or a −1 percent annual inflation rate. It's the same thing.

There are three primary forms of inflation: monetary inflation, cost push, and demand pull.

1. *Monetary inflation.* This is what happens when the government distributes more money than that which is representative of total national output. It does this either by printing more money, through a reduction in required bank reserves of currency, or through an alteration of interest rates that increases spending by people who hold large savings reserves. Not only does a greater ratio of dollars to output mean that each dollar has less underlying production value, but that also means that traders

and speculators will push down the value of the currency, since the total available amount of currency will be relatively higher compared to the amount of volume of currency desired. In addition, more currency in circulation means more spending, which increases demand for goods, particularly consumer goods and short-term production goods associated with investments. This in turn forces companies to spend a greater amount in costs to produce enough goods for everyone that wants them. Some fringe economists refuse to recognize any form of inflation except monetary inflation. They are wrong.

2. *Cost Push inflation.* This is what happens when costs of production increase, forcing companies to raise prices to stay profitable. Sometimes it's the result of spending more to increase production or spending more to maintain production as costs of raw materials rise. This occurs often in the insurance industry: A person's insurance price increases to reflect the costs of their coverage because they make many claims. This kind of inflation also occurs in the price of oil. Damage to oil production equipment that reduces the available quantity will increase prices as companies attempt to recover lost production potential as well as recover from the costs of damaged equipment. Increased costs and prices force workers to demand higher wages in order to continue purchasing goods, resulting in higher labor costs. Some argue that this kind of inflation is only possible if the government increases the money supply, but this ignores the principle of monetary velocity (that is, how frequently a single unit of currency is traded for new goods and services), the role of trade, and the use of credit and lending to fund purchases. The government does not need to print more money if people just incur a greater amount of debt. As we saw during the financial

downturn of 2007, spiraling debt creates huge problems if it's improperly managed by either borrowers or lenders. In addition, cost push inflation resulting from increased costs of imports does not require any shift in money supply to cause inflationary pressures, as that will be caused by the shift in trade flows and the terms of trade.

3. *Demand Pull inflation.* This type of inflation happens when people want to purchase more goods than are available. In these circumstances, either a company will sell to the people willing to pay the most, or the company must spend more money to increase its production capacity. This kind of inflation is very common during periods of high economic strength (also called a boom cycle). Since employment is high, people earn and spend more money, forcing companies to expand their production potential above previous levels.

As with cost push inflation, demand pull inflation can manifest as cost push inflation in a nation purchasing the exports of the nation originally experiencing demand pull inflation. In other words, increased costs and prices associated with high levels of demand in an exporting nation will translate into higher costs for the importing nation without respectively high differentials of demand over supply, causing cost push inflation to occur (this will have a significant influence on trade in the long run, but in the short run this will cause inflationary market shocks). Neither demand pull nor cost push inflation are inherently related to monetary inflation, however.

Any of the three forms of inflation can be reversed to form deflationary pressures. Also note that policies designed to manage inflation and deflation are only able to apply pressure, not directly change the direction of economic growth or inflation.

What You Should Know

So far all this talk about inflation has been purely about domestic economics. So, what does any of this have to do with global economics and trade? The answer is simple: everything!

Let's say for a moment that one nation experiences inflation but its trading partner does not. The volume and direction of trade will shift as a result of inflation. If the price of goods in Country A increases, that has a limited meaning for the people in that country since wages are likely to increase somewhat as well (although usually not as much as prices). However, the wages of workers in Country B, Country A's trading partner, will remain the same, so if the exchange rate between the two nations doesn't change, then the people of Country B must spend more of their own money to exchange for enough domestic currency to purchase the goods. As a result, inflation causes the price of Country A's exports to rise, decreasing demand for these exports and increasing demand either from Countries B, C, and D, or simply increasing domestic purchasing rather than relying on any imports at all. Of course, there are two perspectives: Higher prices for Country A also means more exports for Country B, as Country A has to spend less money as a proportion of its national average to acquire goods from overseas.

This is only a temporary effect, however, as exchange rates adjust. This topic will be discussed in greater detail in topics 33 and 34.

It's important to note that the amount of trade a nation experiences can also influence inflation. If a nation's trade goes up, then the total amount of demand within the nation increases. If this added demand for a nation's goods begins to test the current production levels, this can create inflationary pressures. If the demand for a nation's exports decreases, then this can ease inflationary pressures (although, of course, it can also cause unemployment, if any company or industry relied heavily enough on exports).

Why You Should Care

The influence that inflation has on trade and vice versa plays a critical role in determining balance of payments levels for a nation. This in turn can influence the role that not only an individual company has within a global industry, but even an entire nation. If you or your employer do any sort of business across international borders, it is especially important that you pay attention to inflation rates in each nation where you have operations. It's critical that you at least understand your own nation's inflation and how it changes compared to some of your nation's largest trading partners.

Inflation, in the media and in common public discourse, is always treated as a bad thing. As with most economic matters, where a threat is created, so too there is created an opportunity. The key lies in understanding the implications of inflation on economic transactions and financing. Once you understand what inflation is, and how it impacts transactions, you can take advantage of the shifts that occur. Apply this information on inflation to your own business transactions but be wary, as the impacts discussed here are temporary. Applied to international investing, the influence of inflation and deflation are no different than with domestic investing. You want your returns on investment to exceed annual inflation, or else that inflation will cause the value of your investment to decrease relative to the prices in your nation. As with transactions, however, as we'll see, the role of inflation on international investments becomes a bit more complicated.

33. INTERNATIONAL FISHER EFFECT

By now you might have guessed that there is some relationship between interest rates, inflation rates, and exchange rates, and that it all influences trade between nations. This relationship, in its simplest form, is calculated using the International Fisher Effect (IFE). The IFE, named for its formulator, the economist Irving Fisher, states that for every 1 percent differential in interest rates between nations, there will be a 1 percent differential in the opposite direction between the exchange rates of the same nations. For example, if Vietnam increases its interest rates by 5 percent over Thailand, then the Thai baht will appreciate in value over the Vietnamese dong by 5 percent. While this is a simplified example, it effectively illustrates the relationship between interest rates and exchange rates.

The IFE uses inflation as a mechanism for turning changes in interest rates into changes in exchange rates. As interest rates increase, inflation increases as well, since the increase in interest rates causes cost push inflation to occur as a result of the increased cost of borrowing money. When this inflation increases, then the exchange rate of that nation over another must decrease, in order to correct for the differential of purchasing power parity of the currency and the previous exchange rate, allowing for that nation's exports to retain an equilibrium price on the international market. If that's a bit much to follow, here's a theoretical example.

Belize and Uruguay, trade partners, have the exact same interest rate of 10 percent, the exact same inflation rate of 10 percent, and an exchange rate at BZD1 = UYU1 (BZD = Belizean dollar; UYU = Uruguayan peso). One day on a clear morning in spring, the Belizean government decides to raise interest rates by 1 percent. They think it will be simple, but lo! they start a series of events that alter the economies of both nations. Now that Belize has an 11 percent interest rate while Uruguay still has a

10 percent interest rate, the inflation rate in Belize also goes up to 11 percent! That in turn causes their exchange rate to decrease to BZD0.99 = UYU1! By the time the Belizean government realizes what's happening, their exports to Uruguay have already increased significantly because the people of the land of Uruguay can now purchase so much more with the same amount of UYU!

. . . or can they?

The reality is that the relationship between interest rates and exchange rates is not so easy to control. As of this writing, no one knows how strong a reaction in exchange rate will occur in response to a change in interest rates. There have been instances where there was a reaction greater than one-to-one (the ratio I used in the example above), and there have been instances that yielded less than a one-to-one ratio.

What You Should Know

Part of the confusing nature of the International Fisher Effect is that the influence it has changes over time. Interest rates don't necessarily change and then immediately change back. The differential of interest rates between two nations continues, and since exchange rates are constantly changing relative to each other (except for those that are pegged to each other), what we end up with is a reaction in exchange rates that is continuously responding to variations in inflation and trade that result from the change in interest rates. This reaction to exchange rates follows a commonly seen pattern in economics called a J-curve.

A J-curve is so called because—wait for it!—it's a curve on a graph that looks like a J. What this means for exchange rates is that when a nation's interest rates rise relative to another nation's, its exchange rate does, in fact, decrease for a time but then it increases past its starting point. This happens because the devalued foreign exchange rate attracts more trade, forcing the exchange rate back up over an extended period of time, assuming that the conditions of trade meet the Marshall-Lerner condition (discussed in topic 34).

Why You Should Care

Global economics includes a number of chain reactions where a seemingly innocuous bit of economic policy causes an indirect impact on a number of things that the policymaker had never imagined would have ever been possible. The International Fisher Effect is one of those chain reactions of interlinking economic influences. What's really amazing about the IFE is that, although still unrefined, it starts with a premeditated, predictable action taken deliberately by a member of the federal government. From that point on, you just have to anticipate the different steps in the chain reaction in order to benefit from the process by which it all happens.

34. MARSHALL-LERNER CONDITION

One of the most basic ideas in economics is price up, demand down—that is, the belief that as the price of a product goes up, the quantity of that product that people will buy goes down. While there are exceptions to this rule, generally it holds true. The next step is to determine how much a change in price affects demand. This is determined using a calculation known as the price elasticity of demand (PED). This divides the percent change in the quantity of units sold by the percent change in the price. A PED of 1 would mean that a 1 percent increase in price is correlated with a 1 percent decrease in unit sales; greater than 1 means that unit sales would drop by more than 1 percent, and less than 1 means that unit sales would drop by less than 1 percent.

The Marshall-Lerner condition (named for Alfred Marshall and Abba Lerner) applies this idea of price elasticity to the relative increase in price resulting from changes in exchange rate. It does this by comparing these changes to fluctuations in the balance of trades that result.

Recall that when Nation A's exchange rate depreciates relative to other nations, then Nation A's exports are cheaper for other nations while imports into Nation A become more expensive. As a result, we're looking at two separate PED calculations: one for exports and one for imports.

1. *Export PED:* Percent change in the quantity of domestic goods demanded by foreign nations divided by the price change caused by exchange rate fluctuations. As a nation's exchange rate depreciates, the amount of domestic exports purchased by foreigners will increase as a result of the lower prices using foreign currency.

2. *Import PED:* Percent change in the quantity of foreign goods demanded domestically divided by the price change caused by exchange rate fluctuations. As a nation's exchange rate depreciates, the amount of foreign imports purchased by locals will decrease as a result of the higher prices using domestic currency to purchase foreign goods.

Now add the two values together. If they equal 1 or greater, then the impact will be an increase in the nation's exports and a decrease in imports, causing a positive shift in the nation's current account and a negative shift in the capital account (i.e., this will either lessen a trade deficit or increase a trade surplus). If the total is less than 1, then either demand for the nation's exports won't increase enough, or domestic demand for foreign imports won't decrease enough to reverse a trade deficit. Even if the total is less than 1, demand for imports and exports will still change (assuming the total is greater than 0), but this won't create the positive shift in the current account because the differential in the quantity of trade income needs to exceed the depreciation in the value of the trade income.

What You Should Know

At first depreciation in value of a nation's currency causes little more to happen than a shift in the value of imports or exports, without actually changing their quantity. The reason for this is that it can take time for individuals and organizations to change their spending habits, develop new contracts, and otherwise alter expenditures and sales to react to the shift in exchange rate. It is for this reason that, like the International Fisher Effect, the Marshall-Lerner condition tends to follow a J-curve.

The Marshall-Lerner condition influences the International Fisher Effect if the requirements for the condition are met (the sum of the PED for imports and PED for exports is equal to or greater than 1). Under such a circumstance and the impact on exchange rates that a change in interest rates has as a result of the inflationary mechanism, those exchange rates will increase again over the long run. This will be as a result of the shift of the balance of payments and the underlying increase in demand for the nation's exports as well as a decrease in the distribution of its currency internationally.

Why You Should Care

A change in currency exchange rates between two nations changes the value of business exchanges, but that is neither cause to panic nor celebrate. If your currency appreciates compared to a trading partner, you can get your supplies cheaper, and if your currency depreciates, the things you purchase from overseas will be more expensive. This all happens only in the short term, though, as the businesses in both nations work to adjust their purchases and sales in response to the change.

Once you understand that a change in the value of your country's currency doesn't always affect its balance of payments, you can use the Marshall-Lerner condition to determine in the long term how you and your company should react to a change in exchange rates. Decide how it will influence demand for your product, understand how it will influence your demand for foreign imports, and properly prepare your pricing strategies, output, and even how best to allocate your assets geographically to take the most advantage of the shift in value. For instance, if you have financial assets or investments in one nation, then the change in exchange rate will first change the value of the assets relative to your own currency's rate, but that may change the competitiveness, total production, or even just the total volume of trade and resource flows to influence your assets in ways you otherwise would not have expected.

35. OTHER EXCHANGE RATE DETERMINANTS

There are a wide variety of things that determine the supply and demand for currencies that, in turn, determine exchange rates. A number of the most influential ones have already been discussed: national production levels, interest rates, inflation rates, balance of trades levels, terms of trade, and purchasing power parity. Still there are others to be explored. Some of them cause temporary fluctuations, while others may cause permanent changes.

Permanent changes to the exchange rate of a currency are those that significantly alter the value of the currency as a form of trade. That doesn't necessarily mean that the value of the currency *itself* has changed, but its ability to be traded has somehow changed by the nature of the currency's usage. In contrast, those influences on exchange rate that are temporary in nature don't change the underlying value of the currency, nor do they even significantly change the long-term supply or demand for currency.

What You Should Know

The issue of public debt influences exchange rates but even the most vocal of opponents of government spending and debt seem to have difficulty vocalizing the reason for this. Here's a basic explanation.

Governments incur debt by issuing treasury bonds and treasury notes, meaning that the majority of government debt is held by private investors. As the government spends more borrowed money, a couple of things happen. First, the actual demand for U.S. funds through government spending decreases relative to the supply, requiring the government to spend more money to attract more private contractors. Second, the bad press associated with "record government debt" alienates investors, requiring the government to push up interest rates on the debt in order to attract investors. Recall from our earlier discussions that interest rates have a significant influence on exchange rates, which is what causes the relationship between debt and exchange rates between nations.

Speculative investors are also a determinant of exchange rate. Unfortunately, speculation is easily the most difficult influence on exchange rates to predict. Sometimes speculators seem like little yappy dogs, barking when the wind blows the wrong way. Unfortunately we don't have the opportunity here to delve into behavioral economics, so let's summarize a bit.

People are irrational; their financial decisions tend to change based on their mood at the time, the news of the day, and the potential gain or loss (as opposed to the likely gain or loss). They participate in herd behavior (all of them tend to start "running" in the same direction based on nothing more than seeing others running). This all warrants a lot more explanation, but let's reduce it to saying merely that people are unstable, and that instability contributes to small, temporary fluctuations in exchange rates.

Speaking of behavioral instability, let's talk about confidence! Much of the inherent value that we, as people, place on currency comes from our confidence that we will be able to exchange it for goods and services at a later date. Without that confidence, a currency is worthless.

Nothing harms public confidence in a currency more than political instability. People begin asking whether the current government that backs the currency will exist for long, whether any new government will support the currency, or whether policies that influence inflation and exchange rates will see dramatic changes. On the other hand, governments that are extremely stable tend to have currencies with not only higher exchange rates but also less volatile exchange rates.

The final, and probably most important, of the secondary determinants of exchange rate is the status that some currencies achieve as a reserve currency. Becoming a reserve currency is sort of like being in an elite club; unfortunately, membership in that club comes with a curse.

Being a reserve currency means that demand for the currency goes sky-high and it maintains stability. Reserve currencies are those that are considered to be very stable, have low risk, have low volatility, compose a significant percentage of total transaction value, and can be easily exchanged or offered in just about any nation.

At that point, some currencies are chosen to measure the value of internationally traded commodities, such as oil. For decades, OPEC has used the U.S. dollar to price oil exports; the result is that all nations are exchanging their currency for U.S. dollars, or at least paying an equivalent price to the market exchange rate. Governments tend to hold large quantities of these reserves to make trading and exchange easy for a wide variety of nations. Other reserve currencies include the euro, the Japanese yen, and the British pound.

Why You Should Care

Sure, it's important to know how exchange rates are determined, but these determinants are really just secondary compared to the more influential ones. However, these secondary determinants give vital information about the nature of money and the role that people give it in their lives.

36. THE GOLD STANDARD

Gold has been used for millennia as a currency, melted and then molded to form currency by nations across eastern Europe and much of Asia. One of the many roles that gold plays today is as a currency with a floating exchange rate.

Prior to the nineteenth century, the dominant monetary form in western Europe had been the silver standard. The application of a formal rate of exchange between gold currencies began in 1717. Isaac Newton (who was running the royal mint of the United Kingdom at the time) overvalued gold in terms of silver, causing a drain of silver in the region as people exchanged for gold internationally. By the 1790s, the situation had reached crisis proportions; to correct the problem Britain implemented the international gold exchange system in 1819.

The reason for this short history lesson is to show you exactly how long the idea of a gold standard or silver standard has existed. By the twentieth century, we fixed some of the problems with currency by allowing national production to determine exchange (the original roots of the use of currency) rather than to arbitrarily peg currency to some precious metal. Despite this, there are people who want to reinstitute the gold standard.

At any point in this book where the gold standard is mentioned, understand that although the dates of implementation and popularity of either gold or silver may differ, their actual functionality did not. For the purposes of understanding international transactions I will be referring exclusively to the gold standard, but the two terms can be used interchangeably.

What You Should Know

A gold standard is a method of economic and monetary regulation that pegs the value of a nation's currency to a fixed amount of gold and restricts the quantity of a nation's currency to the amount of gold it has in its reserves. Often this is accompanied by a free exchange of currency and gold by the government for domestic use, though the export of gold was often discouraged throughout history, given that nations were required to maintain extremely high reserves of gold in order to effectively withstand the volatility associated with the supply and demand for currencies worldwide. This, of course, causes a conflict of roles for gold.

Whether you're talking about gold or silver, all these different measures of value are just new ways of saying the same thing: mercantilism (see topic 25). Don't let the existence of a paper currency fool you—as long as that currency is strictly pegged in value and quantity to the nation's supply of gold, it might as well just be using the gold directly.

The nation could have just as easily determined that mud, instead of gold, should be the unit of value underlying a nation's currency and the result would have been the same. National wealth under a gold standard is based not on the nation's ability to produce something of value, but on how much of some naturally occurring substance can be accumulated. Put simply, limiting a nation's monetary policy by strictly tying it to the amount of gold that a nation holds restricts the ability of that nation to properly manage its economy.

In addition to limiting economic growth, the gold standard severely exaggerates recessions (an inability by the Federal Reserve to use expansionary monetary policy was a major contributor to the severity and duration of the Great Depression) and causes short-term price shocks associated with the inevitable changes in the peg or discovery of additional gold, and that's all just the domestic harm.

Internationally, the gold standard suffers from the same basic problem that the U.S. dollar suffered from during the early twentieth century when a large number of the world's developed economies pegged their currencies to it, a problem referred to as the Triffin Dilemma (named for the economist Robert Triffin). This states that when a nation's primary currency also acts as an international reserve currency, there is a conflict between the roles that the currency plays. While this is usually reserved for currencies, remember that under the gold standard, gold is the currency of choice for many nations, which leaves each of them incapable of properly managing their own economy.

For centuries, governments would go to war with each other in order to collect more precious metals, seeing any trade deficit as a loss of national wealth. (This was also the motivation for Spanish voyages to Central America in the sixteenth century; they were in search of large supplies of gold and silver.) It became illegal in many places to pay foreigners with gold or silver, and many governments attempted to stop all forms of international trade.

During the attempt of Western nations to implement a gold standard in the 1800s, all exchange rates were pegged to gold, so when price levels around the nation changed, they all changed together. This caused havoc on the balances of payments between nations, and kept any nation from obtaining its full potential gains from trade.

Basing the wealth of a nation on gold also creates wealth disparities based on nothing of value. Gold is expensive and difficult to process, and not all nations are provided with the same reserves of gold. Under a floating rate, as currently used, a large increase in the supply of gold will automatically decrease gold's price, but under a gold standard that gold is representative of the nation's total wealth. As a result, if an international gold standard were implemented, Australia would probably end up the richest nation in the world since it has the largest natural gold reserves. Not that there's anything wrong with Australia—except that their total production potential is much lower than many other nations.

Milton Friedman, a Nobel Prize–winning economist, estimated that the cost of maintaining a proper gold supply would be 2.5 percent of GNP. For the United States, that would have been $300 billion in 2005. For nations without proper access to their own gold supply, trade would become exceedingly difficult, and even developed nations would have difficulty benefiting from trade with these nations.

Why You Should Care
The gold standard has been rejected on a global level, by every modern nation in existence, for a reason. While it's easy to see

why it might be attractive, as it is extremely simple to understand and is usually associated with low long-term inflation rates, these are really the only two benefits. As noted, those low long-term inflation rates are joined by extreme short-term price volatility, including large economic shocks. The gold standard is also associated with extremely high unemployment and slow economic growth since nations are incapable of performing the monetary changes required to recover from a recession in any sort of timely manner. As far as simplicity goes, as you've probably guessed by now, "simple" economic solutions are often wrong.

The threats associated with mercantilist descendants such as the gold standard are global in nature. There is not merely collateral damage when one nation fails, but multiple nations are directly affected. Nobel Prize–winning economist Paul Krugman said it best in his article for *Slate*, "The Gold Bug Variations": "The current world monetary system assigns no special role to gold; indeed, the Federal Reserve is not obliged to tie the dollar to anything. It can print as much or as little money as it deems appropriate. There are powerful advantages to such an unconstrained system. Above all, the Fed is free to respond to actual or threatened recessions by pumping in money. To take only one example, that flexibility is the reason the stock market crash of 1987—which started out every bit as frightening as that of 1929—did not cause a slump in the real economy." The Great Depression of the 1930s and the Long Recession of the 1870s were both caused, in very large part, by the gold standards of their respective times. Avoiding this in the future should be a top priority for anyone with a sense of self-preservation.

37. SPECIAL DRAWING RIGHTS

When governments themselves want to exchange currency, they use the International Monetary Fund; or at least those 188 nations (out of the estimated 196 nations in the world) who are members of the IMF do so. When governments exchange currency, it's never in small quantities, so there are some special methods by which this happens. Each uses a special type of currency, available only to governments, called Special Drawing Rights (SDRs). Although SDRs aren't technically a currency, it can be helpful to think of them as a special type of currency that has very stringent limitations on how it can be used.

SDRs can be held by any member nation, then used freely in exchange for the currencies of other member nations. Currently, the value of the SDR is set by the average of four currencies: the U.S. dollar, the Japanese yen, the euro, and the British pound. Although the value of SDRs changes as frequently as the four currencies that compose the valuation basket, the basket itself is evaluated and set every five years. In other words, even though the peg is evaluated every five years, the currencies to which SDRs are pegged continue to float, causing valuation fluctuations. As with any pegged currency, the peg itself must be checked periodically to ensure that fluctuations in the value of the currencies to which the SDR is pegged do not cause severe disparities in the market value of the currency and the pegged value.

SDRs are claims against reserve currency held either by the IMF or its member nation. This works in two ways.

1. A nation can purchase SDRs and use them to exchange for the market value of other currencies.

2. If a nation does not have enough reserve currency to meet the requests of the nation attempting to exchange its SDRs, the IMF, which is given the authority by its

member nations to ensure that other nations have reserves of the currency being sought in sufficient quantity so as not to put that nation at risk of having shortages, will exchange its reserves for SDRs in order to fulfill the needs of those nations that are already experiencing shortages.

Neither of these transactions significantly alters the total wealth of a nation; they are merely used as a method of facilitating trade and other financial transactions between nations. The IMF maintains reserve currencies primarily by selling SDRs as well as by charging interest on loans. The exchange of these currencies for SDRs helps to coordinate trade and currency exchanges between nations to promote international trade and economic growth.

What You Should Know

The IMF itself acknowledges that the current role of the SDR is insignificant in global trade. While the IMF attempts to point out that increasing the role of the SDR could significantly benefit global trade and IMF member nations, even those with very large currency reserves, that is not the current reality for the SDR, so we're not going to worry about speculating. What's really important to know about the SDR is the purpose for which it was originally created and the role it was meant to fulfill.

According to the IMF website,

"The SDR was created by the IMF in 1969 to support the Bretton Woods fixed exchange rate system. A country participating in this system needed official reserves—government or central bank holdings of gold and widely accepted foreign currencies—that could be used to purchase the domestic currency in foreign exchange markets, as required to maintain its exchange rate. But the international supply of two key reserve assets—gold and the U.S. dollar—proved inadequate for supporting the expansion of world trade and financial development that was taking place. Therefore, the international community decided to create a new international reserve asset under the auspices of the IMF. However, only a few years later, the Bretton Woods system collapsed and the major currencies shifted to a floating exchange rate regime. In addition, the growth in international capital markets facilitated borrowing by creditworthy governments. Both of these developments lessened the need for SDRs."

In other words, just as attempts at implementing a gold standard failed to simultaneously meet the needs of the domestic economic policy and international trade, so did the use of the U.S. dollar, to which just about every major currency was pegged under the Bretton Woods system.

Why You Should Care

Sometimes it's hard to see exactly how something that's exclusive to the federal governments of the world's nations can influence, or be influenced by, the individual people of those nations. The real importance, though, lies in the role that the SDR currently plays even in a world of floating exchange rates, which can't be fulfilled by our current system of currencies.

The SDR improves international trade in several ways:

- It decreases exchange rate volatility in the trade of large volumes of currency between governments. Some nations have gone as far as to peg their currencies to the SDR.

- The system by which SDRs are allocated and distributed helps to facilitate the exchange of foreign currency reserves to meet the requirements of IMF member nations.
- Nations can borrow SDRs at very low interest rates, stimulating investment and growth, particularly in developing nations.

What does all this mean to you? The SDR acts very much like a currency that mediates trade and foreign exchange cheaply, quickly, and easily. The amount of foreign exchange currency that is available in a nation doesn't just come from thin air. The exchanges that occur between governments and other large institutions develop the infrastructure by which such exchanges become possible in their current form. The SDR, although less important than it once was, still has an important role to play given its nature as an intermediary currency that allows for the easy exchange of both fixed and floating currencies without sacrificing the ability of any nation to maintain proper monetary policy.

38. FOREIGN EXCHANGE RESERVES

Governments hold varying levels of a number of foreign currencies, and some quasi-currencies like gold, in something called foreign exchange reserves. The motivations for doing so are far greater than simply having some extra spending cash, although, in a sense, that is one reason. The levels of each specific currency being maintained are deliberately chosen and changes are made only with careful consideration. As a nation increases the level of its foreign currency reserves, it also decreases the supply of that currency in the open market.

What You Should Know

There are multiple reasons to manage foreign currency reserves. Currency reserves are managed in order to manipulate exchange rates. By altering reserve currency levels, economic policymakers can control the exchange rate to maintain stability by decreasing the impact of fluctuations, shocks, and speculative movements.

In addition, holding foreign exchange reserves, particularly of reserve currencies, helps to facilitate trade between the nation holding the currency and the nation from which the currency was issued. This is good for economic growth for both nations.

Finally, having foreign currencies on hand can serve as an investment. Although maintaining large foreign currency reserves carries a significant risk, it is in our nature to be a bit more bold in our holdings of currencies that are stable or appreciating, while eliminating from the reserves currencies that are depreciating in value or are otherwise volatile in nature.

Why You Should Care

Practically every nation holds some quantity of foreign exchange reserves, yet most people aren't entirely sure why. Knowing exactly what these reserves are used for, why your nation is holding them, and how they influence the value and quantity of currency worldwide is critical to understanding the nature of money in the global economy.

CHAPTER 5

Restrictions on Trade

Regardless of the overall gains and economic improvements that are created through trade, some feel threatened by increased competition from international sources. Both a lack of understanding regarding the overall benefits of trade and the inability of some companies and individuals to adapt to the global economy contribute to public resistance to foreign trade. This resistance puts pressure on politicians, as companies and individuals attempt to influence policy in order to make their own organizations more competitive in the domestic market.

Regardless of whether the motivation for promoting trade restrictions is misguided or self-serving, note that all trade policy set by a government is domestic. While a government can, for example, ban all trade between another nation and its own country, it can't stop other people around the world from trading with the banned nation—except by using political or physical coercion. This chapter is concerned with ways in which governments restrict their own nation's trading practices.

39. TARIFFS

One of the most commonly implemented restrictions to trade is a tax on imports—commonly called a tariff. Tariffs are levied on imports coming into a nation, typically with the primary intention of making them more expensive and thus discouraging people from buying them.

For a long time in Western nations tariffs were a primary source of government revenue; but in the early twentieth century they were largely replaced by other taxes. This allowed governments the opportunity to use tariffs more strategically as a method of managing trade and the economy.

Tariffs are set on specific items coming from specific nations; whole corn is treated differently than milled corn, both of which are treated differently than corn syrup, and so on.

Tariffs can be imposed either on a per-unit basis (for instance, in a shipment of 100 tons of corn, each ton is taxed separately) or by value (based on a percentage of the purchase price).

What You Should Know

Tariffs are set when domestic industries are having difficulty competing with foreign goods. In the short term, this has limited success. If the price of foreign-made goods goes up, people have less reason to buy them. If comparable products made domestically are the same price or cheaper, people will purchase them instead. This gives companies within one's own country a boost, making their prices more competitive compared to goods from other countries.

However, the long-term effect is to prolong economic inefficiencies. Tariffs support noncompetitive businesses and eventually pass on the costs of keeping them afloat to the consumer.

Why You Should Care

If you want to buy something made in a foreign country, you should know whether its price also reflects a tariff the government has imposed on it. If you're a small business owner attempting to export goods abroad, foreign tariffs can have a serious impact on your company.

40. QUOTAS

Quotas can either increase the cost of goods coming into the nation in a manner similar to tariffs, or they can limit the quantity of foreign imports. The former, called tariff-rate quotas, allow a set quantity of a particular type of good to enter the nation duty-free; then any additional quantities are subject to a tariff. The latter allow only a set quantity of a particular good to enter the nation and once that quantity has been reached, no additional imports of that particular good are allowed to enter at all. Quotas usually require the importing entity to obtain an import license for a specific quantity of the goods in question, obtained from whatever government authority is in charge of issuing the licenses. These licenses typically require a fee, increasing the costs of imports.

What You Should Know

Quotas aim to protect domestic jobs; they tend to be more effective at accomplishing this than tariffs, since a quota guarantees a limited supply of a particular import, whereas the price increase resulting from a tariff may not greatly influence demand for the import.

On the other hand, quotas also cause more collateral damage than tariffs. Given that quotas tend to be more effective in accomplishing their short-term goals than tariffs, their impact on cost inefficiencies tend to be greater.

Governments have been accused of distributing import licenses unfairly for political gain. Whether that is true or not, those companies that obtain licenses have a very strong competitive advantage over their domestic competitors. This anti-competitive circumstance allows a few companies to control the entire industry.

Why You Should Care

As a consumer you might not directly feel the effects of a quota. However, quotas add complexity for those organizations that import and export goods. It is not as simple as merely paying an additional fee during the course of business-as-usual. One must be aware of companies that either have import licenses or are frequent holders of such licenses. Those organizations must be targeted for sales rather than merely marketing to all potential customers as one might typically attempt.

Some companies specialize in obtaining licenses and distributing goods between nations. These companies will sell to just about anyone. If you don't mind buying bulk quantities, individuals can save quite a bit of money this way as well, not to mention having access to a wider variety of products.

41. SUBSIDIES AND DUMPING

The opposite of tariffs, subsidies are payments the government makes to organizations to either produce or export a particular type of good. Agricultural concerns are frequent recipients of government subsidies. Farmers produce corn; then the government pays them a set amount for every unit of corn produced.

Sometimes governments provide subsidies on exports, paying people to ship goods overseas rather than sell them domestically.

The purpose of a subsidy is to make the goods cheaper for consumers. The government pays a portion of the production or export costs so that the producer can charge a lower price. However, countries that pay subsidies to export goods are sometimes accused of "dumping."

Dumping occurs when the exporters of one nation sell goods to the people of another nation "below fair market value." The strategy is to force foreign competitors out of business. Some commentators have argued about whether dumping really exists, or whether perceived cases of dumping are merely the result of combining a competitive advantage with a domestic subsidy.

What You Should Know

Although not every subsidy is intended to allow companies to cheaply dump their goods overseas, any good that receives a subsidy and is subsequently exported is sold at a price below what would normally be possible. While this certainly helps a company or industry obtain a greater share of the global market, it is very expensive and not sustainable in the long run. Such a strategy will do little more than force global cost inefficiencies, as those companies that survive will have increased costs and higher prices. When a subsidy gives one nation's companies an unfair trade advantage, sometimes importing nations will impose a tariff roughly equal to the amount of the subsidy; this is called a countervailing duty.

Why You Should Care

One of the primary reasons for trade is to benefit the people of one nation by seeking out sources of goods and services that are cheaper abroad. For a government to subsidize its own companies in order to make them more competitive against foreign firms is a gross misallocation of assets.

42. EMBARGOES

Embargoes are the most extreme form of trade restriction that can be enforced without military intervention. An embargo is a complete ban on trading specific types of goods between two nations. Embargoes on the export of arms and other military goods are quite common. Beyond military goods, though, embargoes on other forms of goods are usually implemented as a result of political conflict between nations, but also sometimes because of health. After an outbreak of Mad Cow Disease in the mid-1990s caused people to fear tainted meat, many nations placed a temporary embargo on British beef.

An embargo completely stops trade. A travel embargo keeps people from traveling to or from a particular nation. A full embargo stops the two nations from having any contact at all. Cuba was under an almost complete embargo by the United States for many years, a policy that devastated the Cuban economy. At last the embargo was eased enough to allow for medical and humanitarian aid to enter the nation.

What You Should Know

For a nation or an industry under an embargo, the only strategy is to find alternative places to buy and sell goods. Embargos can happen without warning, it's impossible to tell how long they'll last, and there's no good way to circumvent them without breaking the law (something that is ill advised).

Why You Should Care

Prior to the U.S. embargo of Cuba, the United States purchased a very large proportion of one of Cuba's largest industries: sugar. As a result, sugar from Cuba was extremely cheap in the United States. As food prices rise around the world, the United States continues to maintain an embargo that has accomplished nothing of its original goals as stated in 1960 yet could help ease food prices in this country by once again allowing for the import of very cheap sugar.

43. VOLATILITY

Volatility is a social and political problem. While not intended to be a trade barrier, it often results in reduced trade. Volatility refers to anything within a nation that lacks a predictable trend, particularly those things that experience wild changes.

If a nation's currency is volatile (in other words, the value of the currency changes dramatically and frequently), many people do not want to be paid in that currency because it may be worthless in the near future. If a nation's government is volatile (e.g., factions struggling for control, violent crackdown on civilians, etc.), then it becomes difficult, and sometimes dangerous, to trade with the country.

What You Should Know

Every nation experiences fluctuations but these are almost always within parameters with little or no risk. The kind of volatility that will restrict trade causes changes that are relevant to the operations of a business or the mechanics of a transaction.

These shifts are frequent enough for their very inconsistency to be predictable.

Nations with larger economies can often minimize volatility by diversifying the types of goods they produce (rather than relying on just a few types of goods that might fluctuate in supply and demand). They also tend to have less social and political volatility as a result of having reasonably ample resources for the people to maintain a quality of life that discourages conflict.

Why You Should Care

Volatility is an indicator rather than a cause of problems. Still, it can be a barrier to trade, and the underlying causes of the volatility must be resolved before the nation can more effectively attract trade. Fixing the problems that cause volatility is a topic more associated with developmental economics, touched on in Chapter 10.

44. COUNTERFEITING AND IP VIOLATIONS

Counterfeiting and violations of intellectual property (IP) law are among the most serious economic crimes in existence. They are closely related, and, sadly, both are widespread.

Brand-name goods that are much in demand will often stimulate widespread production of knockoff versions. These violations create a de facto trade restriction, since high-profile brand companies will often refuse to export to nations with known counterfeiting problems. Counterfeiting reduces not only the number of sales that a company can potentially make but also the value of the original brand, since people associate the inferior fake goods with the originals.

What You Should Know

Counterfeiting often calls up a picture of a guy selling fake Rolex watches out of the back of a van. However, it can dip into larger ethical gray areas. For instance, drugs meant for HIV patients tend to have high prices because research is expensive. Once the drug is available on the market, however, unscrupulous companies can replicate it very cheaply because of the lack of research costs. In Sub-Saharan Africa, where HIV rates are higher than in any other part of the world, imported drugs that could save the lives of millions are too expensive for widespread distribution. However, domestically made generic versions are often well within the price range of those who are sick.

Should foreign pharmaceutical companies export to these nations where counterfeiting is so common, knowing that they are saving lives while still making a few sales? Or should they refuse to sell their drugs to these nations at all because they will be counterfeited, taking away funding for future pharmaceutical research? These questions are not easy to answer.

The popularity of file-sharing programs such as Napster or Bit Torrent, although not as ethically complex, is really no different. For a long time there had been little effort among record labels or movie producers to distribute their media more cheaply. Napster, it could be argued, illustrated that a demand wasn't being met. The result: iTunes. This innovation fueled an explosion of devices to store and play this media, including tablet computers, smartphones, MP3 players, eBook readers, and much more.

Despite this example, companies tend to avoid exporting to nations that have serious counterfeiting problems, seeing it as too great a risk. These companies fail to realize that black markets are natural problems that form from differentials in supply and demand. The solution is innovation.

Why You Should Care

Counterfeiting, IP violations, and (more recently) media piracy are hotly debated. The reason for the confusion is that both sides, in their own way, are correct. Although the potential benefit that companies experience from trade is great, the risk can be equally great. The risk of copyright infringement increases as companies trade internationally. Assessing the degree of risk involved then determining the best way to mitigate that risk is a critical step in trade.

45. INFRASTRUCTURE

Those physical structures, facilities, and connections that make it possible for companies and communities to function make up what we call infrastructure. It's a necessary logistical component that makes interaction and distribution between people possible. Key elements of infrastructure include:

- Roads
- Bridges
- Canals
- Airports
- Electric power grids
- Natural gas and oil pipelines
- Sewer systems
- Irrigation systems
- Coastal management structures
- Dams
- Postal service
- Telephone
- Internet
- Communications satellites

Parts of infrastructure depend on each other. For example, an electrical generator of any sort (e.g., coal, nuclear, wind, solar, etc.) is useless unless that energy can be made available to people on a massive scale. The infrastructure itself, in this case, includes power lines, junction boxes, usage meters, power stations, and, arguably, the staff required to manage the power stations, read the meters, manage the accounting, and everything else that's involved to ensure electricity remains continuously available.

What You Should Know

One of the major problems with infrastructure is that it's expensive to create and maintain. While most infrastructure projects hold the potential to be profitable, the majority are still funded by the government.

In global economics, infrastructure typically refers to three primary things: transportation, communication, and information.

Transportation means that people and objects must be able to move between different physical locations, including shipments of goods between nations. Transportation infrastructure includes airstrips, water ports, roads and freeways, bridges, fuel points, supply points, and more.

Communication and **information** infrastructures overlap because they frequently use the same systems. Some of the most common infrastructures that allow for international communication and information transmission include shipping and mail systems, telephone networks, and Internet availability.

Why You Should Care

Without the infrastructure required for transnational communications and distribution, trade cannot take place. Without the proper trade infrastructure, global economics grinds to a halt. This has been one of the largest challenges throughout history, spurring the construction of the Panama Canal (a project that failed multiple times before finally being completed in 1914), and the railroad systems throughout Africa (which have also been primarily a failure).

46. ENVIRONMENTAL AND CONSUMER PROTECTION REGULATIONS

Aren't laws that protect consumers or the environment a good thing? How can such laws possibly be harmful? Chances are good that you think I'm a schmuck. Hear me out. I never said that environmental and consumer protection laws were bad or good—simply that they restrict trade. Yes, many people think, for example, that making the water safe to drink is a noble cause and one that makes economic sense. But we're talking about trade. Although a government that protects its source of fresh water will have healthy people, it may also increase the cost of production for domestic companies as well as repelling companies anxious to trade us their cheaper water supply.

Is it right for companies to harm customers or the environment with reckless business practices and dangerous products? Some argue that it is appropriate; others disagree. Is it up to the government to create laws that protect us from such things? That's also debated. The only point I'm making here is that these laws do, in the short run, make production more expensive. If a company spends a lot of money making sure it's safely disposing of waste, the cost of its operations increases and it must increase price, making it less competitive in international trade.

What You Should Know

Environmental and consumer protection regulations force companies to adhere to standards that increase costs, limit distribution, and otherwise hinder business. Because these laws differ from nation to nation, two things happen: some businesses are less competitive and some foreign businesses stop exporting their goods.

Whether the laws themselves make economic sense needs to be studied on a case-by-case basis, but any time a business must meet additional requirements in order to continue daily operations, their financial performance is constrained. By the same token, when goods must meet minimum requirements in order to be sold legally, foreign companies also incur additional costs. For years, Chinese-owned car manufacturer Geely has attempted to export vehicles to the United States, but its cars do not meet emissions standards. This restriction directly limited trade.

Why You Should Care

During the early twenty-first century, the dangers of poor consumer protection enforcement in China became apparent as a series of faulty products, including poisoned toothpaste and lead-tainted toys, harmed global consumers. Obviously, such reckless abandon is not appropriate, and proper laws must be enacted to provide recourse for damages done to consumers. However, some still strongly resist such laws.

The trick is to determine whether the law in question creates economic benefit or is being implemented simply as a measure to protect domestic production. It's not an easy task, since nobody actually claims to be supporting laws that are purely self-serving, but it is necessary to understand whether a law is going to hurt you or help you.

47. TRADE WAR

Trade wars occur when two or more nations use trade restrictions against one another to the point that these restrictions become generalized. Nation A places a tariff on goods exported from Nation B; that country feels that this unfairly restricts trade so it issues a tariff or quota on Nation A. And from there things escalate.

Such economic tactics meant to hinder trade between two nations might include any of the trade restrictions mentioned thus far. They also might include specific methods of managing exchange rates and even extend to more aggressive forms of economic combat. In extreme cases, trade warfare spills over into physical warfare.

What You Should Know

The World Trade Organization has been greatly beneficial in limiting not only the number of trade wars that have occurred but their severity. Member nations can appeal to the WTO, which will provide an unbiased analysis of the circumstances to determine whether trade restrictions violate WTO rules. This has helped increase the role of diplomacy in resolving economic conflicts, similar to the goals of the United Nations (although the WTO is better at what they do).

Why You Should Care

Trade wars occur much more frequently than traditional forms of warfare, although they are often resolved in such a timely manner that they can hardly be called wars. Still, the damage that occurs is real. The decision to launch a trade war is made not because it is economically sound but because it is politically convenient. The actual economic impact of those restrictions is harmful to all nations involved.

CHAPTER 6

Managing Global Risk

The world is filled with risk. However, just because something is risky doesn't mean that it should be avoided entirely. Risk is nothing more than a potential cost and must be assessed for both potential maximum loss and probability. There are many types of risk, all associated with different aspects of the global economy, and all of them can be measured to determine whether a particular action is advisable. When managed properly, risk can be both predicted and mitigated; the costs, anticipated in advance as a part of analysis, reveal the expected benefits of expanding globally and how the organization must price its services in order to stay profitable. All important forms of risk are associated with some type of reward. Managing global risk is a matter of measuring the expected benefit against the potential losses and the probability that those losses will be incurred.

In this chapter we'll discuss the different types of risks as well as several common methods for limiting the amount of risk associated with international transactions.

48. TRANSACTION RISK

Exchange rates between currencies go up, down, and move all around in a never-ending dance. Whether you gain or lose any of that wealth depends greatly on which currency you have or are expecting to possess and which way the exchange rates are moving. The potential for a loss of value resulting from a change in exchange rates is known as foreign exchange risk. Of course, just as there is potential for loss from a change in exchange rates, so too there is a chance for gain.

Let's say you own a car company—we'll call it Your Car Company (YCC). You plan to export 100 cars from the United States to England for a total revenue of GBP100,000. At the time you signed this agreement, one U.S. dollar was equal in value to one British pound, so you budgeted for an income of USD100,000. However, by the time the exchange takes place the exchange rate has dropped. One U.S. dollar is now worth two British pounds. All of a sudden, you're not getting USD100,000 anymore; you're now getting only USD50,000.

On the other hand, suppose YCC owns a dealership in England and plans to purchase 100 cars from the United States for USD100,000. If the British pound drops in value relative to the U.S. dollar, you'll have to pay more pounds in order to fulfill your contracted obligation for USD100,000.

In both these situations, you, the owner of YCC, lose money because of the change in the exchange rate. On the other hand, since exchange rates can increase or decrease, it's possible that YCC could make more money or spend less as a result of transaction risk. When a company determines that the exchange rate is going to change and tries to make money by buying currency that is going to go up, this is called foreign exchange arbitrage (arbitrage means taking advantage of the difference in current price and expected price).

What You Should Know

The risk in exchange rate fluctuation is that the currency of exchange loses value and you end up paying more or earning less than you had originally anticipated. Note that in the case of transaction risk, one person's loss is very often the other person's gain. As a result, foreign exchange risk holds both risk and potential. A company may analyze this risk (and many others) to either decrease the amount of loss they experience or increase the amount of revenues they earn.

Companies trying to take advantage of foreign exchange fluctuations typically do so through asset management rather than attempting to do so through their purchases and sales. In other words, many prefer to maintain as little transaction risk as possible since the gain or loss on such foreign exchange fluctuations can be difficult to predict.

Nations that have large, stable economies tend to be associated less with transaction risk. Of course, organizations that participate in significantly large international transactions will be at greater risk for even small changes in exchange rate; those nations with more stable fiat currencies—or currencies where the money derives its value from government regulation—usually experience less volatility.

Why You Should Care

Except between two nations whose currencies are pegged directly to one another, transaction risk is an issue for every transaction that occurs across national borders. As a practical matter, since every time you buy anything, there's a very good chance it was made, at least in part, in some nation other than your own, you're directly affected by changes in the exchange rate.

Most businesses that regularly transact business over multiple currencies account for the expected losses associated with this risk, or at least the costs of mitigating the risk. This is reflected in their pricing strategy, causing the price of the goods you're purchasing to be somewhat higher.

49. POLITICAL RISK

The role of a nation in the global economy is set, in large part, by the government in charge of that nation. The policies of that government define how the nation interacts with others, how companies participate in trade, and the degree of risk that organizations attempting to trade with that nation face. A change in government policy can greatly help or harm not only individuals or companies, but the entire global economy.

For example, it is not uncommon for governments to restrict what is allowed to leave the country. Laws often either limit or completely prohibit citizens (and noncitizens) from taking assets out of the nation in which they currently reside. These are called repatriation restrictions.

Political risk should not be assessed at just the national level. While paying attention to the federal government of a nation can be informative, these smaller governments often have a significant influence on regional economies. While local governments cannot typically set policy related to trade, they can influence trade within their jurisdiction.

What You Should Know

Companies assess political risk based on two primary categories: micro and macro. Micro risk includes the possibility that the government will pass some policy that influences either individual companies or sectors within the nation, or even individual projects on which the organization might be working.

Macro political risk, on the other hand, includes policies that apply to all organizations, often from all nations. These can include trade policies, currency policies, immigration policies, and a wide variety of other actions. In the United States, the Buy American Act is a form of far-reaching policy that represents macro political risk for any foreign company that had previously sold goods to the U.S. federal government (the act requires the government to attempt to source all its goods and services first from U.S. suppliers).

Why You Should Care

Political decisions often have absolutely no economic benefit or at least none that's immediately obvious. This means there is really only one way to manage political risk. Instead of merely accepting that politicians are completely insane, many companies attempt to be proactive in their approach by persuading politicians to include their input in policy decisions. They do this by providing information, consulting in implementation, hiring professional lobbyists, having their executives actually apply for political positions, or making campaign contributions. This controversial but effective approach isn't welcome in all nations because it does not result in sound economic policies.

50. INTEREST RATE RISK AND INFLATIONARY RISK

Interest rate risk and inflationary risk are faced by investors but international expansion actually allows them to mitigate the severity of these risks. This is done by giving investors with international ties tools to transfer assets between the two nations in order to take advantage of the relative differentials in interest rates and inflation rates.

Inflationary risk refers to uncertainty regarding the future real value of one's investments. Say, for instance, that you hold $100 in a bank account that has no fees and accrues no interest.

If left untouched there will always be $100 in that bank account. If you keep that money in the bank for a year, during which inflation is 100 percent . . . well, you've still got $100. Only now, if you take it out and put it in your wallet, you'll only be able to purchase half the goods you could have bought a year ago. In other words, if inflation increases faster than the amount of interest you are earning, this will decrease the purchasing power of your investments over time. That's why we differentiate between nominal value and real value. Nominal value is the total number of units of currency you have, while the real value refers to changes in the value of that money, taking inflation into account. Interest rate risk refers to the amount of uncertainty that interest rates will increase after you purchase an interest-bearing investment.

What You Should Know

In global economics, we're less concerned about interest rates or inflation rates than we are about the differences in these rates between nations. We already know that both inflation and interest rates influence exchange rates, and that can be an important variable when deciding how to manage the movement of your capital assets around the globe. For the moment we're going to assume that exchange rates will stay the same.

When there are differences in inflation rates between two nations, the one with the lowest inflation has the lowest risk. If you have 100 units of currency in each of two nations, and one has 10 percent inflation and the other has 1 percent inflation, your assets will be worth more in the nation with the lower inflation. It doesn't necessarily matter where you hold your assets because the nominal amount of currency won't change as a result of inflation rates (remember: we're keeping exchange constant). But when you use the currency, it will be worth more in the nation with lower inflation. If we now take changes of exchange rate into consideration, we can see that keeping your assets in a nation with lower inflation will be more beneficial because the high inflation will harm the value of your assets when exchanging between currencies.

Differences in interest rates between nations form an interesting dynamic. Typically, within a single nation, you want to invest in bonds that have the highest interest yield for the amount of risk you're incurring. It's common to time these investments so that you buy bonds when interest rates are at their highest and not likely to increase any further. When investing internationally, it's quite possible that the interest rates in another nation could continue to increase past the point at which your own nation's interest rates stop. Understanding both nations not only gives you additional potential for investment gains, but also gives you the opportunity to trade between nations in order to generate the greatest returns.

Why You Should Care

If you're generating 5 percent interest on your investments but inflation is 10 percent, you're still losing 5 percent of the real value of your investments. On the other hand, if your investments in another nation are generating 3 percent return and inflation there is only 2 percent, you'll have higher real value. Since we know that the differentials in inflation and interest rates do, in fact, change exchange rates, you'd gain the greatest benefits by keeping your investments in the nation with the lower interest rates but the highest differential between interest rates and inflation rates.

51. TRANSLATION RISK

When an organization owns foreign operations, lists foreign assets on its books, or owns assets denominated in a foreign currency, any fluctuation in exchange rates between the foreign-denominated assets and the primary currency of the company will alter its book value. By book value, we're referring to the total value of all the assets held by the organization, including buildings, equipment, cash, and stocks.

Let's say, for instance, that you own 10,000 Mexican pesos (that's MXP10,000). They don't belong to a company or other organization; you just have them stored in a coffee can in your kitchen. If your currency (let's abbreviate it URC) is on par with the MXP you've got URC10,000 or MXP10,000—it doesn't really matter which way you think of it. But suppose the MXP increases in value 10 percent compared to your currency. Now your coffee can of money is worth URC11,000 rather than the original URC10,000, plus whatever you can get for the can itself.

That sounds like a great opportunity! Increase your net value by just holding on to foreign money, right? Well, not if you're holding on to URC and living in Mexico. If that's the case, the value of the money you're holding is less than before the change in exchange rate. That's why this is considered a risk.

What You Should Know

As with transaction risk, translation risk is a threat that requires mitigating or an opportunity to benefit. It's a bit easier to do this with assets you already own, because you can keep your assets denominated in another currency for an extended period of time. Since there are no other parties involved (except, sometimes, the bank exchanging your currency) you can more easily switch back and forth between currencies. Still, this can be an extra risky strategy. Many prefer to focus on reducing risk and allocating assets internationally based on the requirements for operations and growth.

As a company develops an ever-increasing amount of foreign assets as a result of expanding operations it places itself at risk to lose company value, particularly if any significant amount of those assets are long-term physical capital such as property, plants, and equipment, which cannot be easily transferred between currencies or countries.

As with transaction risk, those nations that have larger, more diversified, or more otherwise stable economies tend to have lower problems with translation risk. The risk increases with nations that have larger fluctuations in economic production (particularly those that are reliant on seasonal production) and those small or moderately sized nations that have not pegged their currency to a more stable fiat currency or basket of fiat currencies.

Why You Should Care

The real risk associated with currency translation is that the value of a company could, theoretically, drop to nearly nothing with little having changed except an exchange rate. Of course, such a dramatic shift would likely mean that there were some underlying problems associated with the national economy, but the actual operations or competitive strength of an organization need not necessarily change except in terms of financial translation. This drop in value would influence not only the organization itself, potentially harming it beyond repair, but also investors and lenders for that company, and any other stakeholders such as employees, consumers, and, in the case of especially large companies, the economy of both nations. For these reasons it is particularly important for organizations operating in nations that have volatile economies and/or currencies with volatile exchange rates to take special precautions against translation risk for its standard operations.

52. LEGAL RISK

Not every nation on the planet has a law enforcement system that works; nor do they necessarily recognize foreign or international law. When a company has difficulty with a foreign legal system, it's just incurred legal risk. As a rule, foreigners often have far more difficulty than natives with a host country's legal system. That's not always true (many nations go out of their way to try to impress foreigners), but as a general rule it is more difficult for a foreigner than a local to navigate a legal system.

One specific type of legal risk, called settlement risk, refers to a scenario in which an exchange is agreed upon but only one party upholds its obligations in delivering either payment or goods. Across international borders, what recourse does the injured party have? That depends greatly on the details of the contract.

In such a case, if one is even capable of getting a court to take an interest in a case presented by some foreigner, there is the distinct possibility that it will take so long to even begin the process that either the costs associated with the entire process will exceed the potential benefit of pursuing the case or the transaction itself will become outdated and meaningless. As already noted, not all nations have this problem nor will all organizations experience this problem, but this particular form of risk becomes especially important to be aware of because there is little that one can do to minimize the issue once it has already occurred.

What You Should Know

Legal risk comes from a number of sources. First of all, the national legal infrastructure plays a large role. If it's very small, overburdened with too many cases and not enough resources to enforce the verdicts, actions you bring may not be heard. In addition, a weak legal infrastructure gives incentive for con artists and others to take advantage of foreigners.

Another issue that contributes significantly to legal risk is the country's culture. In some nations it is acceptable to take advantage of imbalances in information between the parties to a transaction (colloquially: to rip someone off). Companies must determine how what we would think of as dishonest activity is viewed within a nation where they wish to do business.

The political goals of a government can play a part in defining legal risk. Of course, these goals can create such risk as well. It depends on whether the government has determined that it is in its best interest to protect local companies from unwanted foreigners or whether it wants to attract foreign investors and traders.

Why You Should Care

The most important instrument in mitigating legal risk is the contract. Arbitration can often be a quicker and less expensive process than litigation. Arbitration is handled by a private individual or company rather than the governmental court system. This often allows the process to not only move more quickly, but it is also often less costly than a legal case while still providing a binding judgment. However, while arbitration is binding, little can be done to compel either party to fulfill their obligations.

Another way to mitigate risk is to mandate in the contract that any litigation will take place in the nation with the more responsive legal system. While these preventative measures can help, there is no guaranteed way to eliminate legal risk, and even a positive outcome can be extremely costly.

53. CONVERTIBILITY RISK

Convertibility risk refers to the possibility that a particular currency cannot be exchanged or converted (hence the name "convertibility risk") into another currency. This happens most frequently with currencies that are very volatile—for instance, those belonging to nations that are in the midst of war or revolution, or currencies experiencing hyperinflation or other dramatic monetary problems. Basically, convertibility risk applies to those currencies that are completely worthless outside the nation that originally issued them.

For example, suppose you earned money from working in another nation. You've been paid in that country's currency. Everything's great until the currency changer suddenly tells you they can't exchange the foreign currency you're giving them. Now you're stuck with the wad of money you can't use in any other nation.

What You Should Know

Inconvertibility occurs when nobody wants the currency you have. This happens in two primary ways:

1. The government has prohibited its currency from leaving the country
2. People have lost faith in the currency

The former problem is pretty simple—if the government doesn't want its currency converted into other money, it's worthless to everyone outside the nation. Laws about this are implemented from time to time in nations with volatile economies in misguided attempts to keep assets from leaving them.

When people lose confidence in the currency, that's a much bigger problem—for you and for the government that issued it.

Remember that a currency only has value because people believe that they will be able to exchange it for goods and services. If a nation produces nothing anybody wants, the currency is worthless. If people don't know whether the nation will exist for long or that their production won't continue, no one wants the currency

What can you do with nonconvertible currency? You could hold onto it and hope that it will eventually be traded again. Or you could try to find ways to use it within the nation of origin. Or you could try trading it on the black market, which probably won't get you a great price. But after all, accepting lower value is better than holding onto a large pile of useless money.

Why You Should Care

When you're getting ready to go on vacation, be sure that you can exchange any foreign currency you accumulate back into your home country's money. Currencies that are nonconvertible typically stay that way for a while, so attempting to take advantage of the low exchange value in the hopes that it will increase after it can be converted again is not usually advised. The best way to reduce convertibility risk is to avoid the currency altogether. If you can't do this, figure the expected amount of currency that will remain inconvertible. Once you've determined this, you can measure that potential cost against the money you'll receive from operating within that nation.

54. RISK-FREE ASSETS

For investors and organizations that maintain holdings in a significant amount of assets, particularly liquid assets, expanding internationally can both increase and decrease risk. Although expanding internationally can help to diversify operations, thereby reducing risk, as already noted in this chapter, expanding internationally holds its own risks. One way to limit the risk associated with holding international investments is to purchase a class of financial products called risk-free assets.

Risk-free assets are those seen by those who hold them to have little or no risk of losing value. They include short-term interest-bearing assets, such as treasury bills (or similar equivalent forms of government debt) and timed savings accounts such as short-term or no-penalty certificates of deposit (or any equivalent found within a particular nation). These assets are considered risk-free because they provide a guaranteed percentage interest rate return. That limits the amount of risk of loss associated with more volatile investment assets such as equities but still provides more return than keeping the money in a simple savings account. In addition, these assets are still very short term, unlike bonds, so that there is very little risk of incurring losses associated with increases in interest rates or inflation since they can be withdrawn and reinvested elsewhere, usually within a very short time period.

What You Should Know

Maintaining risk-free assets is a popular way to help companies and investors maintain the value of their liquid assets. At the same time, risk-free assets don't yield high returns; for that you must look to even riskier assets such as equities. All these different forms of investments and asset holdings will be discussed in greater detail in Chapter 7. For now, though, we're concerned about managing risk. In order for organizations to limit the amount of risk associated with holding liquid assets such as cash, investing in risk-free assets can help reduce the amount of risk associated with nations that are experiencing high inflation or exchange rate differentials.

Not all types of risk-free assets are available in all nations, nor are they necessarily always available to foreigners. Timed accounts (which are basically indistinguishable from certificates of deposit) are relatively universal.

Why You Should Care

Each nation manages its own economy and, as a result, each nation has different rates of inflation, interest rates of return, and risk. You can use this to your advantage. Let's say an organization has operations in both Nation A and Nation B. Nation A has inflation of 1 percent and interest returns of 2 percent, while Nation B has inflation of 1.5 percent and interest returns of 3 percent. Assuming there is no change in exchange rates between the two nations, even though Nation B has higher inflation rates that will reduce the value of a constant quantity of assets, it also has interest rate returns that more than make up for the inflation rate. Your best bet would be to maintain your assets in Nation B.

Being aware of risks and opportunities will optimize your value. The returns on risk-free assets are usually very low, so the possibility of using this as a strategy for increasing wealth is minimal, but there are a number of options for limiting risk.

55. INSURANCE

Probably the most common method of limiting risk is insurance. You can insure just about anything: vehicles, your health, buildings, machines, land, specific body parts, antiques, shipments of packages, and even travel. When you insure something, it means that you're distributing the risk of loss among a larger set of people, so an individual who experiences a problem will incur fewer costs associated with the original loss. In other words, you pay a company to take the risk for you.

As far as the global economy goes, insurance does the same thing: It helps distribute the risk that individuals and organizations face. The cost of any loss is paid for by the funds generated by the payment of monthly premiums made by all those who are insured. This helps to manage risk by limiting the total potential loss associated with a single item, regardless of the types and amount of risk it faces.

What You Should Know

Insurance companies profit by taking in more money in premiums than they pay in losses. They do this by carefully (and very accurately) assessing the probability that something will happen to the insured item or person. Then they determine the amount that they will have to pay and place a value on the probability.

Let's say you want to insure an export shipment worth USD100,000. The insurance company knows that shipments from the United States to the location that you are shipping to have a 10 percent chance of being damaged, stolen, or otherwise lost. So, the cost of insuring these sorts of shipments is 10 percent of the package cost, in this case USD10,000. So the insurance company will charge you USD10,000 plus an amount over that to cover their other costs of running the insurance company as well as ensuring a profit margin. Even though you're paying USD10,000, that's still easier than incurring the total loss of USD100,000. That's what makes insurance so attractive in international economics where foreign individuals and organizations often are not given the same rights as local citizens and potential damage is greater.

Why don't people just insure everything they possibly can? To a large extent, we do. Between life, health, property, auto, mail, travel, liability, malpractice, blackjack, and so many other types of insurance, it's common for companies and other organizations—and individuals—to insure every object they own.

Is all this insurance really necessary? That's up to the individual or organizations considering purchasing insurance. If either the potential loss or the probability of an incident occurring isn't great enough, it is not rational to purchase insurance. For instance, it probably isn't prudent to purchase insurance to protect shipping through the Bermuda Triangle, since this is too unlikely to pose a serious risk.

Why You Should Care

A significant difference in doing business in various nations is the degree of risk a company faces. A shipment may be more likely to be attacked in Pakistan than in Switzerland. In that case, you might be more prone to purchase insurance for a shipment heading for Pakistan than one heading for Switzerland. A doctor is far more likely to get sued in the United States than in Uganda, so if an American doctor joins an NGO such as Doctors Without Borders, she's probably safe in decreasing the amount of malpractice coverage she pays for.

56. FUTURES

If you've ever paid any attention to the investment or finance section of your local newspaper, chances are you've heard of futures, even if you couldn't quite make sense of what they are. Futures are a type of contract to either buy or sell a predetermined quantity of a good at a price specified at the time the contract is made. Payment for and delivery of the goods are both performed on the future date set in the contract, or else the contract is settled in cash.

Many types of commodities are sold as futures, including corn, gold, oil, stock, bonds—anything that can be transferred in bulk without differences between units (e.g., one barrel of light crude oil does not vary significantly from the next).

What You Should Know

Futures were originally meant to limit the transaction risk on large quantities of commodity goods by establishing terms for the future purchase or sale of those goods. This reduced the amount of overall volatility in price and cost over longer periods of time. Futures are also now used as speculations in order to generate income. Since the value of goods increases or decreases between the time the futures contract is signed and the settlement date, brokers and investors trade them at prices above or below their original value both to generate income on the final settlement as well as to create income by reselling them at a profit.

The reason the futures are so easily traded is that they are standardized. Each contract out of 10,000 futures of light crude oil will be for the same quantity of oil per contract, the same quality, and so on.

Why You Should Care

When traded internationally, futures are an effective way to limit foreign exchange risk. Thanks to their standardization, futures allow organizations to respond to foreign exchange risk incredibly quickly and, if necessary, resell the futures. This ability to very quickly turn cash into futures and vice versa is called liquidity; the more liquid an asset is, the more easily it can be turned into cash.

The high level of liquidity inherent in futures allows organizations and individuals to remain flexible in their risk management strategy, but what types of risk are they hedging against? The majority of futures that require the delivery of physical goods are based in commodities: energy, mined goods, agricultural goods, and a number of other types of large-volume homogenous assets. These types of futures help to hedge against transaction risk and translation risk.

Even world currencies are available for exchange in tradable futures contracts. This decreases the amount of risk associated with holding a particular currency during a time of inflationary or exchange rate depreciation. Finally, when used to guarantee future exchanges at a current rate, futures can help to alleviate some of the costs associated with interest rate increases.

57. FORWARDS

The primary difference between a futures contract and a forwards contract is standardization versus customization. Whereas futures contracts are standardized, making them easily bought, sold, and traded in large volumes, forwards are customized. A forwards contract generally has the same basic components as a futures contract; the contract states the quantity and type of goods to be delivered, the price that will be paid for the goods, the date of delivery, type of currency that will be used, denomination of valuation, the exchange rate (if applicable), the jurisdiction for legal resolutions should conflict arise, and much more. The primary difference is that all these different components do not necessarily have to follow the same terms, quantities, durations, or any other variables that would make each forward identical to the next. Forwards contracts, in contrast to futures, are typically agreed upon between two parties, and the contract will remain between those two parties throughout the life of the contract, without one side or the other selling or trading their rights to the agreement. This allows people to customize forwards contracts just so long as both parties agree to the terms and the terms are legal within nations in which each of the parties reside.

What You Should Know

In global economics, forwards are frequently used to make large or frequent exchanges while eliminating the amount of risk associated with the volatility of exchange rates. It is very common for organizations that are party to large transactions to agree to the transaction in advance and then execute the contract at a later date or in stages. Because of the range of varying terms in these contracts, it is necessary for the majority of operating exchanges (as opposed to investing exchanges) to resort to forwards.

Why You Should Care

Forwards are extremely common among businesses that participate in international trade. Remember that such trade is not confined to large corporations and governments; small businesses and even individuals engage in it as well. When a shipment is going to be large enough that the cost of purchasing the forward is less than the potential change in value of the goods between the time that the agreement is made and the exchange is executed, companies generally purchase the forward. This process, more than most forms of risk management, helps a very large number of people and organizations to limit transaction risk.

58. OPTIONS

As the name implies, options are a type of exchange contract that gives someone the option to either purchase or sell their assets at a predetermined rate and quantity. The holder of the option can decide at any point before some future date whether he wants to exercise his option (meaning use it) or let it expire.

What You Should Know

There are two types of options: call options and put options.

1. When someone purchases a **call option** he is given the right to purchase a specified quantity of goods at an agreed-upon price as long as the option is exercised before its expiration date. For example, if someone from Venezuela purchases a call option on 100 units of Russian natural gas at a price of RUB100 per unit (RUB = Russian ruble), he can purchase all 100 units at a price of RUB100 at any time before the option expires, no matter what the actual sale price of Russian natural gas or the exchange rate between RUB and VEF (VEF = Venezuelan bolivar fuerte). If the price of gas goes up, or the exchange rate on the RUB goes up, the option holder benefits from exercising the option instead of just purchasing the natural gas. If the price of gas goes down or the exchange rate on the VEF goes down, the option holder would do best to let the option expire and purchase the natural gas at its current market rate.

2. A **put option** gives the person who purchased it the opportunity to sell his goods at a given price and quantity, regardless of what happens to the actual market price of their goods, so long as the option is exercised before

it expires. From the time the person purchases the put option, should the market price of the goods go down or the exchange rate become unfavorable, the holder should exercise his option and sell his goods at the price specified in the option. If the market price increases or the exchange rate changes favorably, he should let the option expire.

Options are frequently used as a method of risk management because they limit the amount of increased costs or lost revenues. Even though options cost money, the amount is very small compared to the potential risk, particularly in volatile economies. The risk factor can be great even in stable economies when dealing in goods that experience dramatic price fluctuations, such as natural resources.

Why You Should Care

Anyone can buy options. Banks, corporations, small businesses, and even individuals can buy, sell, and trade options in any number of things. As already noted, businesses can hedge the risk of international transactions using options to limit losses resulting from variability in exchange rate and inflationary differentials between nations. Options are also frequently used to limit the amount of risk that individual people experience when investing in stocks. Options and other investing derivatives have gained a reputation for being extremely risky, but that's really only when people use them in a risky way. When used as they were intended, as a risk management tool, options hold no more risk than the price you paid to purchase it.

59. FOREIGN EXCHANGE SWAPS

Swaps are a seemingly simple but ingenious device for mitigating the potential for transaction risk, translation risk, inconvertibility risk, and many other risks rooted in the potential for currency to lose its value. Foreign exchange swaps occur when two organizations, each holding different currencies but not necessarily their primary currency, agree to exchange an amount of those currencies that they agree to be equal in value. At the same time, they also sign a forward contract to exchange the currencies back again at terms both parties agree will be fair for the future values of those currencies (which may not necessarily be the same rate). The bottom line here is that a foreign exchange swap means two organizations trade currencies with the intention of trading them back again in the future.

The funds used in a swap are most frequently loans, so the principal and interest repayments must be taken into consideration. When two organizations are trading currencies in a foreign exchange swap, they typically trade cash flows on both the principal and the interest on their respective currencies. This means swaps are subject to interest rate risk.

What You Should Know

The reason to participate in foreign exchange swaps is to maintain a reserve of a foreign currency, usually for use in operations when an organization is experiencing a temporary shortage of funds. That was the original purpose of foreign exchange swaps when they were officially introduced by the U.S. Federal Reserve in 1981. It remains their primary motivation today.

When employed to limit risk, swaps are used to alter the proportion of assets held in different currencies or anticipate a future need for foreign currency, holding the potential to limit transaction risk, translation risk, political risk, inconvertibility risk, and more. They can also be used to generate income when the investor anticipates changes in foreign exchange rates and speculates on movements by agreeing to terms in a swap they believe will benefit them. However, this is relatively rare.

Foreign exchange swaps are not the only type of swaps available. Other types include credit swaps, commodity swaps, and more, but for the purposes of risk management in global economics, foreign exchange swaps are easily the most important. Still, the most common form of swap, the interest rate swap, can also be performed across multiple currencies, allowing for potential benefit in hedging risk for those organizations with operations across multiple nations. Interest rate swaps allow organizations to exchange the cash flows from the interest rates on different loans, usually swapping the difference between fixed and floating rates across different nations. Interest rate swaps can also span multiple currencies, allowing them to be used in a manner similar to foreign exchange swaps, but focusing exclusively on the cash flows from interest payments.

Why You Should Care

Swaps are used for exchanges with a relatively high value. Unless you are in charge of the finances of some company or you manage a particularly large set of investment assets, odds are you won't ever become involved in a swap of any sort. The reason that organizations should care about swaps should be obvious: it helps reduce the amount of risk. Swaps have less relevance for individuals.

When properly used, swaps reduce the overall costs that organizations face by reducing the amount of loss when certain risks are realized. That means these organizations are either more profitable, can charge lower prices, or possibly both. In either case, anyone who has a stake in the well-being of these organizations benefits, including customers, employees, stockholders, and the community.

60. BARTERS

In some circumstances it's easier to forget about money altogether and just trade goods. This eliminates some of the risks and costs associated with traditional forms of international transactions but creates other challenges. When a transaction takes place wherein each party to the transaction agrees to exchange some value in goods or services instead of using currency, this is called a barter exchange.

This method of exchange has varied in popularity. For a period it became extremely popular because barter transactions were not taxed the same as traditional sales in many nations, regardless of whether the companies generated an increase in net value. Once governments discovered this tricky tax tip, all transactions that changed the value of the company were treated as gain or loss of income. Afterward, barter fell out of favor for an extended period until the fall of the Soviet Union and following financial collapse of many ex-Soviet states. For a number of years, particularly in Russia, barters became a very popular option for businesses as well as for individuals as the nations' economies recovered from the turmoil of the 1980s and 1990s.

A number of large companies operate exclusively to facilitate barter trades between tens of billions of business transactions. Some of these companies focus on retail consumer markets, including swap meets, trade centers, and the like. On an international scale, barter organizations focus on corporations participating in much larger exchanges.

What You Should Know

Barter exchanges are typically used in modern times as a way to avoid the risks associated with transaction risk, inconvertibility risk, and some types of political risk, or even to avoid the costs of currency exchanges. Here's an example of a transaction that takes place in a country whose currency is inconvertible:

- Company A: A foreign company that wants to sell electronics to Company B
- Company B: A domestic company that wants to buy electronics but has nothing Company A wants
- Company C: Can give goods to Company A in exchange for goods from Company B

Assuming all three companies can come to an agreement on the value of exchange, this barter has just bypassed the use of currency entirely, avoiding those risks involved with foreign exchange and holding foreign assets.

The problem with barters is that they can be difficult to arrange. Since they become more common during times of economic volatility, it can be hard to calculate the exchange value of the goods to be traded. As well, the parties must either be in need of goods from each other or they must be able to find a third party willing to facilitate the exchange. The more parties that enter into the agreement, the more complicated it is to work out the details of the contract.

Why You Should Care

Barters present a valuable alternative to traditional forms of exchange. Particularly for the huge percentage of nations that have volatile currencies, barter can make trade possible while managing fluctuations in production or the exchange rate.

It is this very usefulness for limiting risk during periods of economic volatility that has increased the barter trade to $10 billion in 2008, according to the International Reciprocal Trade Association (a governing body for international barter systems). This is despite transaction fees that can reach as high as 15 percent. That many companies are willing to pay these fees means they find it extremely beneficial to participate in barter. After all, a sale worth EUR1 million is only valuable if one receives the money in a manner that is usable.

Since those nations that have a high percentage of barter trades are more likely to be those with very low production costs (given that a highly volatile economy often contributes to low production and high unemployment), participating in a barter system can also help open the door into nations with high advantages in labor costs but which sometimes don't have use for their own currency. For instance, in Germany between World War I and World War II it was not uncommon for workers to ask to be paid in food rather than in money. Inflation was so high that the money would not purchase as much food by the evening as it had in the morning. In such cases, barter can be tremendously beneficial not only for maintaining good trade relationships between organizations, but also for increasing economic stability within the nation itself.

CHAPTER 7

Foreign Investment

Recall from Chapter 3 that there are two sides to every exchange involved in international economics: the transition of goods and the transition of the ownership of capital. We've talked a lot about the exchange of goods, but much of the focus on capital has been merely on currency. Sure, the majority of capital exchanges that take place are in currency, and we've already established that the willingness to exchange one's goods and services for another nation's currency is a form of investment with the expectation that the foreign nation's currency will maintain or increase its value in the future. Even so, this is only one form of foreign investment.

The majority of foreign investments can be divided into two classes: business investments and financial investments.

1. *Business investments* refer to the degree to which an organization (usually a business, but not necessarily) integrates itself into a foreign nation, especially in the sourcing of capital and the amount of direct involvement with the foreign nation (as opposed to working through partners or through import/export).

2. *Financial investments* work quite similarly to standard financial investments (i.e. stocks, bonds, portfolio analysis, etc.) but with a few added twists that come with the additional complexities associated with transnational capital exchanges.

61. FOREIGN DIRECT INVESTMENT

Foreign direct investment (FDI) is made by an organization or person from one nation into a foreign nation's economic production. It either establishes new operations in that nation or purchases a direct share in some operations that already exist within the foreign nation's borders. These are not investments in the way you're used to them—say, through purchasing stock. The intent of FDI is not to simply invest in the finances of a foreign company, but to invest in its operations and have a role in the production and management of that organization. It is a way for organizations and entrepreneurs to expand their operations beyond the borders of their home nation.

FDI comes in a wide variety of forms, each with its own set of pros and cons. Generally speaking, the primary difference among them is the degree to which the investor is committing herself and her organization to the foreign nation's production. It's possible to have a presence in a foreign nation without actually ever having official operations there. As a rule, the more direct involvement and ownership one has in the foreign expansion investment, the more one has an increased degree of control and ability to remain responsive. That also comes with additional costs and risks associated with the complexity of operating in a foreign nation (not to mention operating in at least two nations—the home nation and the host nation—at once).

What You Should Know

There's an old saying: "No guts, no glory." If you take the additional risk in your investments, you should expect additional returns. It's true that, keeping everything else equal, if an investment has higher risk, people will expect more benefits, but that doesn't mean they're going to get them. There has to be something there to make them believe that the investment will be successful. During the 1990s and 2000s, many companies attempted to expand their operations into China thinking that because there were so many people in China their investment was destined for success. They thought to themselves, "Well, there's risk in this investment but China is so big that there will be a huge payout!" They were wrong and they paid for their recklessness. On the other hand, those companies that actually researched the Chinese market and measured their risk and potential returns, investing responsibly and with prudent risk management, were able to generate the benefits they sought.

Why You Should Care

Once you've performed your proper research and developed an understanding of the risk and expected returns of an investment, the actual process of FDI is quite simple. Often it's no more complex than starting a business in your home nation; there's a bit of paperwork involved, you have to run around to various government agencies regarding permits and registration, and it can sometimes take a bit longer than you'd like, but the process itself isn't really that much different. In some cases it doesn't even take that much; you just have to look up whether or not there are any trade restrictions between your two nations for the particular goods in question, and that's typically available on the Internet or can be found with a single call to your national customs agency.

The point is that foreign direct investment is not necessarily a large and expensive process available only to the largest organizations in the world. Any schmuck with a bit of management experience can do it. The difficult part of FDI is the same part that's difficult in any business: the process of running the business itself.

62. IMPORTS AND EXPORTS

The most basic, easiest, and least risky method of investing in the global economy through FDI is to import and export. Despite widespread use of these terms, people often feel intimidated by the idea of participating in international trade. Importing and exporting is simple and, in fact, there's a good chance that you've already participated in one such transaction.

Exporting, in its simplest form, consists of putting something in a box, taking it to the post office, and mailing it directly to the purchaser. Importing is even easier, since it only involves going to some website, ordering a product, and waiting for it to arrive. Even determining whether there is some law or tax placed on imports and exports is a simple matter; you need to call whatever agency is in charge of such matters and ask them the process for reporting the trade.

As an example of a company that does importing and exporting to another nation without actually maintaining a foreign operation in the nations they are dealing with, I turn to my alma mater, Madonna University. Their school of business has an online option, so they can provide services to foreign students without actually having any operations located abroad. It is an export of services.

What You Should Know

The willingness to export to customers overseas or to import from other nations isn't in itself a foreign investment. With simple imports and exports, the investment really comes in the form of marketing, research, and otherwise making the connections required to make your efforts in trade viable. There is an additional degree of difficulty involved in managing international operations for imports and exports; you have to develop branding, advertising, distribution, and other forms of marketing, and because you are so far away you must handle all that virtually—by phone, Internet, letter, or representative. Importing is much easier; you just have to make sure you're getting the best price possible from all those potential suppliers around the world.

Importing and exporting have the lowest risk of any form of foreign direct investment, the lowest costs associated with international expansion, and still have value not only in decreasing costs and increasing your market size but also in establishing a presence in foreign nations. In order to strengthen your presence in a foreign nation and to manage your company as a primary market choice competing with local firms, or when an exporter is one of your primary suppliers, you'll need stronger forms of FDI. Still, import and export is a form of international investment that even self-employed individuals can afford.

Why You Should Care

Odds are a very large percentage of everything you purchase in a given year is imported from another nation, in whole or in part. At the same time, at least a portion of whatever you do for work contributes to the value or facilitation of some export. With the advent of the Internet, global marketing and sales have become easier than ever, and expanding yourself or your business internationally can lead to a dramatic increase in the financial and operating efficiency of the organization. For people and businesses searching for cheaper alternatives than what's available domestically, importing is an available option that is no more difficult than searching the Internet. For larger volumes, more valuable shipments, and continuous need, it might be helpful to contact foreign suppliers directly or meet with foreign consulting firms that specialize in foreign market analysis. For producers or retailers, selling domestically is no longer even a requirement if they can establish a large enough Internet presence. Direct advertising abroad can establish one's company quite well within the market.

63. PARTNERSHIPS AND JOINT VENTURES

When two or more people own a single organization that is not incorporated—it doesn't matter if each owns an equal share or not—it's called a partnership. A partnership either forms a new organization or else it turns a nonpartnership organization into a partnership.

Partnerships, in global economics, usually refer to organizations in which at least one partner holds residence in a different nation. It does not typically refer to a scenario where an organization, established as a partnership between people all living in the same nation, attempts to expand into a different nation; that's considered a wholly foreign owned enterprise.

Developing a foreign partnership is often seen as the next level of foreign direct investment. By entering into a partnership you commit to only partial ownership of a foreign company. That still involves a greater degree of involvement and association with that foreign nation's economic operations. It does not involve integration with other foreign organizations and does not require you to accept the entirety of the risk involved in developing the foreign enterprise. The upshot is that partnerships are still safer than some other forms of FDI.

Joint ventures are similar to partnerships, except that instead of individual people, one or both of the partners are organizations.

What You Should Know

In global economics, partnerships are useful for a few reasons. First, going into business with a foreigner who is already familiar with the foreign market, culture, and business environment can be invaluable, especially if you're not already familiar with those yourself. On the other hand, teaming with someone who has business or industry expertise or is willing to provide funding can also be helpful.

Some governments do not allow foreigners to own businesses within their nation, or restrict foreign ownership in a particular industry. This can be overcome by entering into a partnership with a local partner.

Developing a foreign partnership does, however, present some risk. You should be particularly careful in choosing your partner and in establishing the contractual details of your relationship. Hiring a lawyer who specializes in the laws and legal system of the nation in which the partnership will be established is highly recommended. One common way to develop a partnership in a foreign nation is to purchase or invest in a share of an already existing foreign company (noncorporation, of course). This can help to take some of the uncertainty out of the startup process and assist with many of the questions about the credentials of your potential partners.

Why You Should Care

Foreign partnerships afford certain benefits over a simple import/export operation. Maintaining a presence in the foreign nation allows the company to be more responsive to changes in the market and better manage the operations related to the foreign competition. Partnerships, as one enters into a foreign nation, integrate the organization more fully while still allowing the foreign partners to mitigate the risk of completely integrating into a nation not their own.

Note that both partnerships and joint ventures usually extend to all forms of organizations (although partnerships where one partner is a corporation tend to be exceedingly rare).

64. MERGERS AND ACQUISITIONS

A merger occurs when two organizations combine to form a single, larger organization. An acquisition is similar, except that one company actually purchases the other, giving one company total control over the other.

Expanding operations through mergers and acquisitions (M&A) helps to take a lot of the uncertainty and risk out of FDI, which is why they are so popular. By merging with or acquiring another organization that has already established its operations in a foreign nation, it is very simple to determine whether that company has been successful in the past and whether their competencies and operations will complement those of the acquiring organization. Since the company is already established, that also eliminates a lot of the risk and uncertainty associated with a startup, since the organization has already gone through the legal hurdles, developed a customer base and distribution channels, and is recognized by the nation in which it operates. That allows foreign companies, through the use of M&A, to expand internationally while minimizing risk.

What You Should Know
Mergers and acquisitions are confined to large companies, at least when they involve international companies. It can be a very

expensive, difficult, and long process even within a single nation (it should come as no surprise that buying an already successful company is not cheap), without the added complications of performing such transactions across multiple nations. So, while much of the risk associated with a startup is eliminated, organizations take on those different risks when engaged in an M&A deal. That includes uncertainty about management and corporate culture (employee turnover in M&A companies is often very high), complementary operations (things may not work as you'd hoped), branding and product lines (they may cannibalize each other), and even the true value of the company being acquired. To be blunt, if you wouldn't merge with a company when it was operating in your home nation, why should you merge with it overseas?

Why You Should Care
The 1980s marked the point when the use of M&A as an international expansion strategy gained popularity. The influence these exchanges have on the global economy can be far reaching, as both companies rearrange their operations, strategies, and resources. Jobs frequently change location or importance; assets change location; operations within the organization are rearranged; purchases that the company makes change; and their sales demographics change. A single M&A deal can dramatically change the trade and asset movement between two nations. The larger the companies party to an international M&A deal are, the more those two nations have become increasingly economically integrated. As more companies own one another across borders, the more integrated do those nations become as a result of the economic codependence caused by the share of ownership each has in the other's economy.

65. WHOLLY FOREIGN OWNED ENTERPRISE

The decision to open a wholly foreign owned enterprise, or WFOE, is about as big a commitment to the economy of a foreign nation as an organization can make. A wholly foreign owned enterprise is a company, division, or branch that is located in one nation but is entirely owned by an organization, individual, or set of partners who claim citizenship in another nation. Unlike other forms of organizations, a WFOE does not share ownership or control of the organization with any foreign entity, even those that reside in the nation in which the WFOE is being established. Instead, the investors have decided that they're savvy enough to take on the challenge of expanding internationally on their own and will assume all the risk as well as all the rewards associated with the investment. To summarize, a WFOE is an organization in one nation, owned by another nation.

There are a number of benefits associated with a WFOE, mainly the increased control and strategic consistency, as opposed to those of partnerships or mergers. In contrast to import/export, establishing a WFOE allows an organization to much more closely manage the organization's role within the foreign nation. WFOEs tend to be easier to create and dissolve than partnerships and ventures. More than any other form of FDI, starting a WFOE allows nations to keep their operations private, more closely manage their distribution channels, and otherwise protect their company and products from copyright infringement or corporate espionage. It is for these reasons that the WFOE is probably the most common form of FDI.

That's not to say a WFOE is all great, either. There is a substantial degree of risk involved any time an organization tries to expand into a foreign nation. Anyone who does this should hire foreign nationals at all levels of management and operations.

Many governments require that a minimum percent of the labor force be citizens of the nation in which the WFOE was established.

What You Should Know

The majority of foreign direct investment is made up of WFOE-style organizations. Each one faces issues that are often unique to its industry, but there are a number of concerns that all WFOE companies encounter. We've already talked about the legal restraints that some nations implement, as well as familiarity with the local community. The concept of *guanxi* in China, for example, means that people rely heavily on personal relationships for their business decisions. It's a little bit like the old saying, "It's not what you know, it's who you know that matters," except *guanxi* is more deeply ingrained within Chinese culture.

Why You Should Care

Despite the challenges that come with starting a WFOE, this is still well within the capabilities of the vast majority of people. It takes a bit more time and effort, but if you start it like you're starting a business, you should be fine. Assess every detail of the foreign nation and its culture; assess the market for your organization; build a brand new business plan and marketing plan; and make sure you study those distinct issues found only in global economics such as the dynamics of currency movements, tax and interest differentials, and capital movement and trade laws.

66. FINANCIAL INVESTMENT

In contrast to foreign direct investment, companies make financial investments without intending to become involved in the operations of the company. Financial investors may purchase debt, equity, or a number of other potential products that provide funding for a foreign company to use for startup costs, expansion, or standard operations, but these investors are given no actual role in the management of the organization; their role is to provide financing in return for a future stake in the organization's profitability.

There are four primary forms of financial investment:

1. Debt
2. Equity
3. Commodities
4. Derivatives

There are other options available, but, particularly for foreign investment, these are easily the most frequently used. Since derivatives are discussed in this book in the chapter on risk management, we'll skip over that and instead focus on equity, commodities, and debt investments. All three are issued with the intent of providing funding for an organization (governments, companies, etc.) and are frequently traded in markets. The person making the investment wants to get back more money than they invested. As we already discussed, the expectation of return is also accompanied by risk. The exact nature of that risk depends on the investment.

What You Should Know

1. *Equities* are shares of ownership in an organization—essentially this is a fancy name for stock. As with all stock shares, your goal as an investor is to either reap dividends based on the company's profits, or sell the stock to another investor at a higher price than you paid for it. Equities carry some risk—rather than rise in value, they may fall.

2. *Debt investment* may sound a little odd to some. If you've ever been in debt, imagine that debt from the perspective of the person who gave you the money; for them it's an investment because they will get back more money than they gave you thanks to the magic of interest rates. Most debt investments are traded in the form of bonds, which often yield interest payments at regular intervals, and always increase in nominal value after the maturity date of the bond. At this point it can be exchanged for the higher value rather than the value paid for it. Again, there are risks associated with these such as interest rate risk, default risk (where the organization goes bankrupt), or inflationary risk. Debt investments can also be traded on a market like stocks, bought and resold at a profit.

3. *Commodity investing* works in a similar way to stocks, except you're purchasing an ownership in the production of a particular volume of goods. Let's say that Peru has a crop of potatoes ready to be harvested in six months. You want to lock in your price, so you purchase ownership of five tons of potatoes now. You can buy, sell, and trade shares of this ownership until the date of delivery for the potatoes. Then you exchange your commodities for the potatoes themselves, or for the difference in cash.

Why You Should Care

Investing in these different financial investments internationally is not so different from doing it domestically. Expanding your investments internationally, though, can very quickly increase the complexity of your investing strategy. There are a number of benefits from diversification, widening your pool of potential investments (or, if you're with an organization, widening your pool of potential investors), and improving the prospects for finding growth investments. There are also unique risks.

With improved technology, international trades in investments can easily occur from any place on the planet. And, not surprisingly, it's become commonplace.

67. INTERNATIONAL DIVERSIFICATION

For both investors and businesses, expanding internationally is about far more than simply trying to generate more income—it's about minimizing risk for the business that can result from economic volatility, seasonal fluctuations, and domestic variations in demand and price. No matter how well an investor spreads out his assets or how well a company diversifies its product line and target markets, there's still the risk that the economy will experience a generalized loss of value, a recession, or contraction. This is called market risk, and many believe it can't be minimized through diversification. On the other hand, not all nations experience economic fluctuations at the same time or even in the same direction. As a result, when an investor or company expands internationally, they are doing more than seeking out more customers and cheaper suppliers; they are seeking out investment opportunities in nations that will experience economic cycles different from their home nation.

What You Should Know

The success of international portfolio diversification can be measured with several instruments:

1. *Beta.* This measures how far from the larger national market your own investments deviate. In other words, if the market increases 10 percent and your portfolio increases 10 percent, then your beta is 0. If your portfolio increases by either 2 percent or 18 percent, your beta will be either high or low. Beta isn't a measure of volatility; it measures only how far from average a particular investment or portfolio strays.
2. *Rf.* This refers to the rate of return on risk-free investments (remember that from the chapter about risk?). Investors want to exceed this rate of return, regardless of whether they're investing in FDI or financial investments.
3. *Rp.* This refers to the rate of return on a company's product portfolio or an investor's investment portfolio. This is the rate of return they are actually experiencing. It should not only exceed the rate of return on risk-free investments but also be high enough to make the risk worth the differential in the rate of return.
4. *Risk.* There are a variety of different ways to measure risk, and just about every financial expert and economist has their own way, some better than others. The risk of loss is not just volatility, as measured in beta, but the risk of your operations or investments actually losing long-term value or failing completely.

There is one thing that I have to make clear: Diversification cannot limit the risks associated with being stupid. It won't save you from the consequences of poor decisions. If you know that some investments are better than others, construct your portfolio accordingly. Diversifying your market or investment portfolio simply for the sake of diversification will result in unnecessary inefficiencies. Look at the best options available for expanding your portfolio and make the best choices you can.

Why You Should Care

Diversification is important for everyone active in the market. Investors can increase their returns by using international diversification to limit the risk of a single investment losing value. Companies can benefit from international diversification by limiting the impact of generalized national economic fluctuations, seasonal fluctuations, and the potential for sudden drops in demand for a particular sector or product. However, even though international diversification can decrease volatility and certain forms of risk, it is not a replacement for knowing what you're doing.

68. EUROBONDS

Eurobonds do not necessarily have anything to do with Europe. Rather, they're bonds held in one nation and subject to its interest rates, but denominated in a currency other than the primary currency of that nation. So, for example, a bond that is issued by banks out of the exchange market in Bahrain but is denominated in Japanese yen and held by a citizen of Morocco would be considered a Eurobond regardless of the fact that it has no connection to Europe.

Eurobonds are named after the currency in which they are denominated. For instance, a Euroyen bond is a Eurobond denominated in Japanese yen; a Eurodollar bond is a Eurobond denominated in U.S. dollars. Each of these bonds can be issued anywhere in the world other than the nation that uses the currency in which the bond is denominated.

What You Should Know

From the perspective of the organization issuing the bonds, Eurobonds offer flexibility. They allow organizations to maintain their debt valuations in a single currency. This not only helps reduce the amount of risk associated with exchange rate fluctuations but also simplifies operations for those companies that don't typically use other currencies or that are looking to avoid transaction risk. This also helps to widen the pool of potential investors, making it easier to attract investors at lower costs associated with yield and interest rates.

For investors, Eurobonds often have smaller par values—or face values—than other forms of larger international investments, making them available to a wider range of investors. They allow investors to speculate on exchange rate fluctuations in addition to the interest generated from the bond itself.

Why You Should Care

The Eurobond is an investing product that is uniquely the product of the global economic community; it's a combination of traditional bonds and currency differentials, intended for global availability. Globalization is producing innovation in some new and interesting areas, and there are likely to be more such products in the future. As for the bonds themselves, they provide a method for investors to speculate on the exchange rate market while mitigating the risk of loss, thanks to the returns experienced in interest rate yields, and without necessarily making investments of gigantic volume. In other words, Eurobonds make the foreign exchange market more accessible to a wider range of investors.

69. SOURCING CAPITAL GLOBALLY

As organizations are integrated more fully into foreign nations and their respective investment markets, as well as the fully international investment market, more options become available to source capital. The vast majority of businesses in the world do not necessarily need access to so many different markets to source the capital they need. Still, there's no reason that even the smallest companies should simply accept higher costs associated with sourcing capital domestically when with a little research they might find that they can achieve their goals more efficiently.

Companies that have been successful on a domestic stock market sometimes think that the next logical step is jumping into a foreign market. This couldn't be further from the truth. There are a number of intermediary steps that integrate a company into the foreign global capital pools.

What You Should Know

No one likes to play guessing games when it comes to large sums of money. The best option when exploring the possibilities for the international sourcing of capital is to start slowly and evaluate each of the steps, as well as discuss a plan with a professional familiar with the markets. Here are a few of the most common steps taken by organizations in their pursuit of more or cheaper sources of capital, in order from least global to most global in nature.

- *International Bond Issue.* The easiest way to begin exposing one's organization to the international capital market is to issue bonds in foreign nations or on the international markets. This method has the lowest degree of complexity, is cheap, easy, and just about anyone can do it.
- *Eurobond Issue.* The next step—a little more complex because of the nature of the contracts and the scarcity of bond markets participating—is Eurobonds. The currency denomination issue makes these bonds a little more complicated than standard international bonds, but they're well within the grasp of even many small businesses.
- *Cross-Listing.* Cross-listing means that a single company has decided to make its stock available in multiple nations' stock markets. This is the first step in expanding one's stock market potential, in order to garner awareness and performance measures in foreign markets without risking driving down the domestic share price.
- *Foreign Issue.* If there is enough demand for your company's stock, then actually issuing shares in a foreign country can help raise significant capital and, if you're lucky, even drive up share prices in your original nation of listing.
- *Euroequity Issue.* Truly the most integrated, most promising, but most difficult to attempt of all the methods of sourcing capital is the issue of euroequity. A euroequity issue is one in which a company holds an initial public offering that is available in multiple nations simultaneously. Investors around the world fight for the same set of stock shares, making for a competitive market.

Why You Should Care

Even the largest companies, when expanding their search for capital internationally, will use investment bankers. It's not so much that the process itself is very difficult, but planning the best options available to you and how to maximize your availability of low-cost capital will go best if you make use of a person familiar with the international markets.

Once the plan is set, the company should make an assessment regarding the costs of sourcing capital purely domestically compared to sourcing capital internationally. The difference in the cost of sourcing that capital means an improvement in your total financial performance, which can make a significant difference in whether your organization is competitive or not.

70. INTERNATIONAL PORTFOLIO OPTIMIZATION

Diversification, which we talked about previously, applies to foreign direct investment as well as financial investment. In addition to choosing the best companies to include in their portfolio, investors have several other ways to optimize the returns on their investments. Generally speaking, as the amount of risk increases so too do the rates of return. Normally, in a domestic market an investor can invest more and more until the rate of risk begins to increase faster than the expected rate of return. These investments, in volume, will either begin to push up the price of individual investments, reducing the rate of return experienced for each additional unit of investment, or the investor will have to begin diversifying into investments that generate lower returns than the best possible choice. In order to optimize the portfolio in a domestic market, then, an investor must continue to add to her risky investments until the point that the best investment she can choose increases risk more than the expected rate of return. At that point, she'll choose to invest in the risk-free options instead.

International optimization changes the potential dynamic between risk and returns in several important ways. In addition to the diversification already touched on in this chapter, there are other variables: The nation that an investor chooses, the relative changes in growth between nations, the currencies that each nation uses, and even the level of economic interdependence between nations all play significant roles.

What You Should Know

In an international investment market, the increase in investment options greatly increases the potential for a portfolio. There are more companies available, many representing better investing options than the second or third best options available in the domestic economy. In addition, the greater volume of investments available means investors can allocate a greater amount of assets to those best options without influencing price and, as a result, the rate of return. This means that investors can generate much higher returns before risk begins exceeding the rate of return, reducing the need for reliance on risk-free assets.

In international investing it's critical to be knowledgeable about the nations in question. Investors often are attracted to "emerging markets"—code for developing nations. Since these countries tend to have economies that grow faster overall than developed nations, it's assumed that any successful company in a developing nation must be destined for an amazing future. To a certain extent, that's true. Investors who can pick out which nations are growing the fastest in a stable manner, and then pick out the best companies in those nations, will reap benefits not only from the company but also from generalized economic growth. Many countries are highly interconnected, however, and so part of the trick is determining how well the economies of two nations match each other. Economic influences are not just domestic anymore; the performances of investments around the world are oftentimes all linked to the same variables.

Why You Should Care

As you might imagine, international investment portfolio management can be a very complicated issue if one allows it to be. Every investor has his own method and approach to investing, some more successful than others. Whether you're a math dork like me, a behavioral analyst, an experienced business tycoon, or just a lucky guesser, you're still only trying to figure out the best value among a series of variables: company, country, and currency. That puts international investing well within reach of anyone that has some extra cash in their pocket.

71. GLOBAL COST OF CAPITAL

Expanding investments and investing internationally isn't just beneficial for investors; it does a lot to help the organizations raising capital by issuing the investments in the first place. All organizations have to deal with the costs of raising capital. Investors aren't going to simply give money away to organizations without some expectations of a benefit; the benefit investors receive is, from the perspective of the organization, a cost. In the case of bonds, this cost comes in the form of interest and yields, while for equity it comes in the form of dividends.

When a company issues equity or debt investments around the world, or at least in one additional nation, it is decreasing the costs associated with raising capital. This occurs because the company has broadened and expanded its market for potential investors. The increased volume and variety of potential investors allow the company to attract an equal amount of capital more cheaply than would otherwise be possible, or to attract more capital than would otherwise be possible for an equivalent cost.

What You Should Know

The potential for the cost of capital to decrease as a result of the international expansion of capital sourcing depends greatly on the firm itself. It's up to the company to extract capital from those international investing markets at a lower cost than domestic ones. The real question lies in the rate of return that a company will be able to generate. If a company pursues a higher budget associated with international projects, it will need to raise a larger amount of capital. It'll cost more to raise this capital than it would if the company were engaged only in domestic projects. In short, there's a tradeoff between raising capital internationally and maintaining a strong return on investment.

Why You Should Care

Lower costs and improved returns for firms translate into more efficient resource usage. This generates either higher investment returns for shareholders or lower costs for consumers—something we'd all like to see.

CHAPTER 8

Movement of Capital

This chapter deals with the most fundamental forces in global economics. As economics is a science that studies how people distribute a limited supply of resources, global economics is, at its heart, the study of how those resources travel around the world.

When discussing the movement of capital, we're not just referring to transporting goods back and forth. Throughout this chapter we will discuss how cities are born and reborn, how people migrate across borders both natural and artificial, the influences on where we locate different types of things and different types of people, and the logistics of how it all happens.

72. TRADE GRAVITY

In the vacuum of outer space, thanks to gravity, objects that float around will be attracted to each other—even very small objects. Every object in the universe exerts some gravitational pull. As these tiny objects cling to each other to become a single object, the gravity of this aggregated object increases, attracting even more matter. This is how the stars originally formed—astronomical amounts of hydrogen gas clustered together in clumps so massive that the hydrogen atoms were forced together, making helium as well as other heavier elements that formed planets and even people. As the late astronomer Carl Sagan said, "We are all made of star stuff."

The same kinds of processes that formed our universe also created cities; they are the basis for a method of measuring capital movement called trade gravity.

Every individual has the ability to attract trade, in the same way that every molecule has the ability to attract other molecules. This is our "gravity." Any person who can produce more goods than they will use can trade their surplus for other goods. When two or more people are producing more together than they could by themselves, they have even greater gravity because they are now producing even more surplus goods than they need. As the quantity of goods being traded and the quality of life increases in the area as a result of trade, other people will be attracted to the center of trade. These people move around the trade region, entering and leaving it, just as the molecules within a star interact with each other.

The interaction of hydrogen molecules in a star produces heavier elements, most of which are eventually expelled from the star. In the same way, the interaction of individuals in a trade region produces goods and services, which are eventually all pushed outward. Just as stars die by shedding their gases, cities shed all their wealth and assets from the middle, forming ghettos, blight, and becoming decayed versions of their former selves.

Trade gravity is a measure of the degree to which an economic mass, usually a city, will attract trade from other parts of the globe. As the economic mass increases, trade gravity also increases, attracting more trade. For example, New York City has more economic mass than Yellowknife, Canada, and as a result, attracts more trade. Economic mass is measured by GDP, which is an imperfect but reasonably useful measure for our purposes.

What You Should Know

The trade gravity between two locations is measured by using the equation

$$F_{ij} = G[(M_iM_j)/D_{ij}]$$

Where:

F_{ij} = the amount of trade between location i and location j

G = the gravitational constant of Isaac Newton, reinterpreted for economic use

(M_iM_j) = gravitational masses of location i and location j, multiplied together

D_{ij} = the distance between the two locations

Put simply, as two locations have larger economic mass, they will attract more trade to each other, but the distance between them will also influence the amount of trade. More distant locations will experience less trade than closer locations of equal economic mass, although this is becoming less relevant with increased globalization. Of course, this is a simplified model. More complex models have proven accurate in predicting trade as well as explaining the development and growth of today's modern cities.

Why You Should Care

Next time you're flying across the country, watch the ground below you as you pass over farmland, mountains, deserts, cities, and suburbs. You'll notice as you get closer to cities that population density—people and buildings—very slowly begins to increase, as if they are in orbit around the central city. The farther away from the center you go, the more space there is between these "objects," until the land becomes wide spaces of farmland or otherwise uninhabited spaces with occasional speckles of farmhouses. Between these more massive objects are fleets of trucks, planes, and sometimes boats that travel back and forth with shipments destined for one city or the next. These vehicles mostly travel between the larger towns and cities, bypassing the smaller entities almost entirely.

This is how the world of people is made. Trade gravity is what allows industrialization and urbanization to occur and makes growth and development possible. Trade gravity is the most basic premise of capital movement out of which our modern world of global economics formed.

73. INDUSTRIALIZATION

When people cluster together, producing and trading, the focus of a region's production capabilities shifts away from agriculture. Primary goods such as agriculture, natural resources, and the production of other naturally occurring assets are still critical for producing goods. If any of us began to starve, we'd probably stop what we were doing and try to grow some food. Fortunately, a single farmer can feed a great number of people—provided he has the tools he needs. It's from this need that industrialization begins: the workforce comes to include people whose primary production function is in making secondary goods, which are manufactured rather than produced from natural sources.

Such manufactured goods improve the quality of life for people, providing comfort, health, and education, further increasing their production potential and giving them greater wealth accumulation through additional trade.

The primary source materials of industrialization are natural resources and human resources. Natural resources refer particularly to high-utility goods that make it possible for those who process them to trade a high percentage of their total production. For instance, corn yields far more edible food per unit of effort by Farmer Jones than he consumes. Farmer Jones sows the corn, waters it, and, eventually, harvests it. He easily fulfills his own needs (and that of his family) for corn and produces a sizeable surplus. In contrast, palm trees yield little food relative to the amount of work it takes to extract it. In consequence, the surplus generated after all that effort is quite small, if it exists at all. This is the reason we eat much more corn than palm hearts and coconuts.

What You Should Know

There are three broad categories into which all economic production falls: primary, secondary, and tertiary. For production of one category to become prevalent, public need for the prior must first be met—primary goods must be adequately produced before production of secondary goods can become anyone's primary source of production, and so on.

- Primary goods are produced from natural sources— food, metals, stone, animals, etc. These are the things that allow us to eat, build shelter, make clothes, and meet our most basic survival needs. Until these needs are fully met, people will pursue primary production. However, let's suppose that in a small village two or three farmers can readily produce enough food for everyone . . . provided they don't have to make their own tools. That works out fine, because now other people in the village can focus on producing farm tools the farmers need. In exchange, the farmers give the toolmakers a portion of the food they've grown.

Together farmers and toolmakers produce more than they could separately, and now one group (the toolmakers) is producing exclusively secondary goods. Assuming their secondary needs are being met, they can move on to tertiary goods.

Tertiary goods aren't really goods at all—they're services. These are often considered the least necessary for survival but the most important for development. Services include teaching, research, defense, and other interactions necessary to improve economic development.

Now that we understand the requirements of trade growth, we need to attract the people who will be involved in the trade. As explained previously, that's the role of trade gravity. Once people and trade meet in a single point (a marketplace, bazaar, trade center, or any other form of centralized meeting place), this trade is what allows industrialization to occur.

Why You Should Care

Industrialization is the process by which a modern nation forms. Our cities grow from smaller centers of trade, developing industrial areas that specialize in manufacturing goods, which are then sold in commercial areas (retail and other forms of distribution, by the way, are tertiary goods). It's all within easy reach of those residents who migrated from other places to work producing manufactured goods and trade for other goods. These relatively small points, geographically speaking, are divided by a patchwork of farmland that is still the fundamental source for sustenance. That is where the global aspect comes into play.

Industrialization requires the movement of resources. Trade gravity draws people to epicenters of trade; businesses produce here; people live here; all the trade between companies and individuals happens in these cities.

Industrialization isn't about human resources, though, even if attracting workers is a natural outcome of industrialization. Instead, industrialization is the process by which physical capital assets are drawn to industrialized areas. Raw materials are brought primarily into these manufacturing-based, densely populated regions, then distributed as secondary goods in proportions that tend to follow the density of the population. This redistribution of resources across vast regions into concentrated points for production allows for increased growth (increased production) and development (increased quality of life).

As we develop new methods of production, the amount of surplus goods produced increases, allowing for increasing specialization of labor, increasing trade surpluses that produce wealth, and increased total resources available among an equal population. This increases the assets that can be allocated to improving life rather than merely surviving (although it doesn't always work that way).

74. URBANIZATION

Whereas industrialization focuses primarily on the movement of physical assets such as machines, raw materials, and the like into concentrated industrial areas, urbanization is the process by which people are attracted to these same regions and become concentrated in them. As trade increases the number of jobs available, the companies seeking workers will continue to offer better wages and benefits until the people of the surrounding areas move to the centralized location of trade (a.k.a. the city). People from smaller towns will tend to move to larger ones, attracted by better wages and working conditions.

Cities date back to the third or fourth millennium B.C. People, by nature, are social creatures, and we are drawn to other people in order to gain mutual benefit from each other. In large enough numbers we change the landscape with our dwellings.

Urbanization comes in two forms: high density and low density. High density urbanization is often associated with cities where people live closer together in apartments, condominiums, or lofts. However, the problems associated with such congestion lead people to seek lower-density urbanization in the form of suburbs.

What You Should Know

On an international scale, national borders mean little regarding the migration of people or goods. Just as capital will cross borders as investors and businesses search for new markets in which to sell their goods or purchase supplies, people will cross national boundaries to seek out opportunities for work.

The centralization of trade exchanges and industrialization that occurs in urban areas allows for not only working opportunities, but also causes increased prices, which tend to increase the cost of living. For example, New York City has experienced much higher regionalized inflation than Omaha, Nebraska. Omaha has much lower wages but also much lower prices. The result is something of a contradiction: People are attracted to the city because of better working opportunities, while others leave the city in search of a lower cost of living. There is, inarguably, a greater diversity of work in urban areas than in rural ones, as increased specialization and industrialization require a higher variety of full-time roles.

No matter where people are in the world, though, these motivations remain the same. Governments try to limit this movement, creating a black market for labor.

Why You Should Care

People move to a city for jobs; people move away from a city in order to cut costs and find an allegedly higher quality of life. Investors buy up as much property as they can in areas beginning the urbanization process because of the increased value of property. When all this is applied to an international level, some unique dynamics are created.

National borders aren't always effective in controlling the movement of people once the economic influences have already been set in place. The development of cities, changing comparative economic growth, and cost and wage differentials do far more than government policies to alter the direction of migration. Within cities, similar linguistic and cultural groups tend to cluster. For instance, one portion of a city may have heavy Korean influence and another might have heavy German influence. This increased exposure to other peoples promotes a wider variety of differences among people, giving urban areas more liberal political ideas compared to their rural counterparts.

75. URBAN SPRAWL AND DECAY

The high concentration of people and capital isn't necessarily a desirable outcome. It brings with it a number of problems: pollution, noise, congestion, regionalized inflation, and much more. In fact, those who can afford it often move away from urban areas. The most direct result is the formation of suburbs, mostly residential areas of people who can afford to move away from the congestion of the city but remain close enough to work there. As the metropolitan area continues to expand, the ability of the city to attract people and resources diminishes. In other words, the trade gravity of the urban and industrialized regions lessens, and as the city continues to expand outward, its assets will shed, blown away like the outer layers of a dying star.

The geographic expansion of a metropolitan area into what was previously farmland is called urban sprawl. While there are no objective measures to determine when an urban area reaches the "sprawl" stage, there are consistent traits among sprawling cities that can be used as a checklist:

- Single-purpose zoning
- Low-density occupation that includes wide spaces between buildings and a significant proportion of single-floor buildings
- Dependency on vehicle ownership resulting from a wide geographic distribution of daily needs

The process by which the urban areas that once attracted people and capital now repel those production inputs, causing the city to lose value and production potential, is called urban decay. Without people to maintain the city, resources, or the income that can be taxed to support and facilitate city maintenance, entire regions of the city will fall into disrepair or decay.

What You Should Know

Urban sprawl and urban decay perpetuate each other. As a city expands, the parts that originally attracted people and assets start to fall apart and become ghettos. As the poverty and disrepair associated with ghettos turn to crime and blight, people and companies move further away from the cities. This is a natural part of the process of regionalized economic growth, the end of a city's life, but it is one that is manageable.

Urban sprawl and decay represent the part of the life cycle of economic growth; resources move away from their cities of origin in pursuit of more lucrative opportunities where growth can occur once again regardless of international borders. As a result, those cities that are hardest hit by these problems are those with a comparative disadvantage in the industries currently operating within their limits. Consider the difference between Detroit, Michigan, and Los Angeles, California. Detroit's primary industry was automobile manufacturing, an industry of primarily low- or moderate-skilled labor that could be performed more cheaply outside the United States. Detroit, which was already experiencing an extreme degree of urban sprawl, lost the majority of its economic resources. By contrast, the primary industries of Los Angeles are those in which the United States has a comparative advantage. Rather than being subject to the full extent of urban decay, Los Angeles actually continues to attract workers, in part through international migration from a low- to a high-income region (discussed in topic 76).

Why You Should Care

The movement of capital is a zero-sum situation. When one area loses people and capital, another area gains those resources. Many people don't want to move to a new town, and some will refuse to learn a new career. While the latter situation can't be avoided, the former is manageable, but it requires an understanding of global economics and the mechanics by which capital moves.

Often during development projects a single area will see a government injection of resources that does nothing more than rearrange the location of wealth; new trendy "hot spots" displace impoverished populations who must now move as property values increase. New construction removes cheap housing, and new ghettos form elsewhere in the same city. This arranging and rearranging of assets within a single city helps to sustain a minimal degree of urban maintenance but does little to resolve the problem.

76. INTERNATIONAL MIGRATION

International migration is a very emotionally charged political subject in many nations. Before we jump into its causes and effects, let's get some terminology out of the way.

Emigration occurs when a person leaves his own nation; *immigration* occurs when a person enters another nation. In other words, it's the same thing but from different perspectives. A *migrant* is someone who leaves her home nation to live in another nation either temporarily or permanently. An *expatriate* is someone who leaves his home nation to live in another nation either temporarily or permanently. The only difference between the two is connotation. The term expatriate typically describes someone from an economically developed nation who moves to a less developed nation. Migrant usually describes someone from a less developed nation seeking a better life in a nation with more economic development.

Legal migrants are those who travel between nations with the consent of both countries. Illegal migrants cross borders without permission. Some nations restrict people from entering their nation; others restrict people leaving. Refugee status is sometimes extended to the latter, often based on political considerations.

What You Should Know

People move between nations in order to receive something they could not get in their home nation. Perhaps it's new jobs, new customers, cheap labor, natural resources, a partnership—

any number of things they can't find at home. The things that motivate people can vary significantly but there are trends. Migrants' motivations can be discerned by looking at their home and host nation.

The majority of migrants move from nations with lower income to countries with higher total income. With better working opportunities comes a better quality of life. When artificial barriers are put in place to restrict that migration, just as when trade restrictions are implemented, a black market forms; in this case, illegal migrant labor. In many cases people move from one country to another seeking a better, more stable quality of life that avoids political or social volatility or other forms of injustice. This was the case with migration from Germany prior to World War II.

Why You Should Care

The exact motivations for migration vary, but they all result from an incompatibility between what is being sought and what is available. It is the existence of this disjunction that allows the problem of migration to persist as well as fueling the black market for labor.

Let's talk for a moment about the border between the United States and Mexico.

People in Mexico often want to move to the United States because of the higher income available; usually migrant workers intend to send a portion of that income back to Mexico. Opponents of illegal (and even legal) migration argue that these workers are competing with American workers for a limited number of jobs. However, in order to compete with migrant workers for those jobs, American workers would have to accept a pay cut. Obviously they don't want to do this. It is that competition for jobs, though, that increased market competitiveness for goods made in the United States, making it an economic "superpower."

Compare this to China's economic growth since the 1970s. China's expansion is fueled primarily by people migrating from farm regions who are willing to accept jobs for very low wages. It's this huge labor force that gives China its production potential. What if we split China into two nations, dividing the cities from the farmland? Chinese companies would now have to draw a huge percentage of their labor force from the ranks of migrant workers. They would be competing with locals over a limited number of jobs.

The bottom line here is that when we open up a border and allow workers to freely cross it in search of jobs, the average income either increases or decreases in order to reach a new equilibrium.

We can conduct an interesting thought experiment by asking whether the removal of minimum wage laws would reduce migration. If companies weren't forced to pay a minimum wage to people, would they still hire illegal immigrants, or would there be enough laborers willing to work cheaply that employers would not risk federal penalties for hiring an illegal migrant? The answer is that migration would decrease significantly, but that poses another question: Is that a scenario that people will accept? The answer—at least in the United States—is, "no."

77. WESTERNIZATION

"Westernization" is the most prominent example in the nineteenth and twentieth centuries of cultural appropriation. Before Westernization the popular term was Europeanization, and after Westernization we were given Americanization.

Anytime a nation exports its goods, or people from that nation migrate to other places on the planet, its culture is distributed along with its goods and people. As other people are exposed to the bits and pieces of a foreign culture, they often adopt those bits. Sometimes it's the novelty of something considered exotic. For example, in many Western nations it's considered trendy to wear Chinese characters on your clothes or as tattoos. In China, though, it's considered trendy to wear clothes with English words on them.

The exposure one people has to the culture of another people occurs almost exclusively through the movement of capital and people driven by that capital. As people travel from country to country, they tend at first to cluster, seeking out others with a common linguistic and cultural heritage. (Think, perhaps, of Chinatown in California and New York, or perhaps of Chaoyang District in Beijing, which boasts a huge percentage of foreigners.) Gradually this breaks down, and the population becomes more integrated.

What You Should Know

The spreading and adoption of culture happens for two primary reasons: function and aesthetics. Either way, underlying economic forces drive the spread of culture.

1. *Function.* The methods and ideas that drive the processes of organizations spread quickly if they are successful. For example, the profit-driven productivity of the assembly line, as popularized by Henry Ford in Detroit's automotive industry, was a cultural icon of the early twentieth century. The success of this method quickly spread to other nations; Japan adopted the idea in its own automotive industry more successfully than in America and

overtook the United States in automotive production efficiency. In the late twentieth century, the American automotive industry looked to Japan for ways to improve its own methods and become competitive. The spread of ideas across cultural boundaries allows for the evolution of an idea by framing it into a new culture. Like a virus that travels the globe, ideas can become something almost entirely new by the time they return to their starting position.

2. *Aesthetics.* Once people are exposed to a novel idea, it can grow in popularity beyond small niche markets. Returning to Japan, for many decades in the United States their animation was almost unheard of. As relations between the two nations grew and more people were exposed to Japanese cartoons, anime grew in popularity. Now, not only does the United States import a huge amount of animation from Japan, but American producers of animation are developing products in anime style.

Culture spreads because there is demand for the goods and services of other nations. This increases competition and creates new preferences in aesthetics, allowing companies to profit from these new markets.

Why You Should Care

The spread of culture, especially Western culture, is a phenomenon that concerns many commentators. There has been an outcry that the increased popularity of McDonald's is destroying traditional food and agricultural industry, contributing to unhealthy eating habits, pushing traditional farmers out of work, and replacing the original food production methods of many regions. Not all change is good, the argument goes.

There's a deeper problem. As cultures interact and merge, we start to see a cultural homogeneity across national boundaries. Many fear this endangers standards in art, music, literature, and other fields culturally unique to different nations. The concern is that by expanding cultural exposure, we are destroying cultural variety.

While this is a valid worry, so far the world appears large enough to continue breeding new ideas, beliefs, and preferences that will generate their own dynamic cultural variations over time.

78. CAPITAL FLIGHT

When capital moves away from nations it's called capital flight. Specifically, capital flight refers to a rapid flow of capital out of a nation, although it can also mean a slower but systematic outflow of capital. Capital flight is usually associated with one of two things: a differential in domestic economic policies that presents a clear opportunity for investors and companies to generate more income or incur fewer costs in a different nation, or naturally occurring economic differentials that also present such an opportunity. The capital in question can be investments, money, entrepreneurship, physical assets, inventories, machines, and just about anything else that isn't directly attached to the country itself. For instance, diamonds can move across international borders, but a diamond mine can't.

As with most things in international economics, capital flight doesn't necessarily refer to just capital leaving a nation. It can also have to do with the flight of capital from a state, province, city, or even an individual district within a single city.

What You Should Know

When an opportunity for greater profits presents itself in another nation (or geographic area), companies and individuals will follow that opportunity. The business may want to decrease costs or investors may want to increase their returns on investment or improve income. Many things can change the economic dynamic between two nations, making one nation more attractive than the other. But all this comes down to one motivation: increasing wealth. It is, after all, the intention of nearly all businesses and investors to make money.

Why You Should Care

The consequences of capital flight can be devastating. As companies move their assets away from a nation, they take with them jobs and production that contribute to the nation's economic growth and trade potential. They take with them wealth that is associated with a successful business and the potential for existing businesses to grow, for new businesses to form, and for innovation or research to be funded. Capital flight thus poses a serious risk of harming the overall economic health of a nation.

79. BRAIN DRAIN

Whereas capital flight occurs when investments and physical assets move away from a nation, brain drain means the departure of highly educated or skilled people. These people have specialized knowledge, skills, or experience that cannot be easily replicated, making them highly valuable. Their departure often results in a lack of people to train new skilled workers, a lack of new development and innovation, and a lack of nationwide technical prowess.

The ability of a nation to develop and produce new or advanced technologies, processes, or other outputs that require a highly specialized skill set is critical to that country's ability to maintain international competitiveness and the kind of market responsiveness required for economic growth. Such jobs often include scientists (both physical and social), professors, engineers, mathematicians, and physicians and others in the medical field. The flight of these skilled people occurs when they emigrate or when students and workers go abroad for school or jobs and neglect to return.

In the early twentieth century China suffered a significant brain drain. Many students were sent abroad to study and bring home new knowledge and skills; many did not return. Others left to escape the civil war between the Kuomintang and the Chinese Communist Party. In the 1960s, as a result of the anti-intellectual movement known as the Cultural Revolution, many educated Chinese fled abroad. Even today, decades after extreme social, political, and economic reforms, this brain drain continues, albeit in modified form. The Chinese still rely very heavily on unskilled or low-skilled labor, and outsource their need for technical or otherwise highly skilled workers.

What You Should Know

People change nations either to escape domestic limitations or to pursue foreign opportunities. In many cases throughout history, those with specialized skill sets had the opportunity to escape their home nation preceding a time of conflict. Many people tried to leave Germany and the surrounding areas prior to and during World War II, but those who had specialized knowledge or useful skills, such as Albert Einstein, found many more nations willing to welcome them than did unskilled refugees. Similar instances have occurred throughout the former Soviet Union, eastern Europe, the Middle East, and parts of the United States.

The other reason for brain drain is the pursuit of opportunity. When people leave a nation in pursuit of better opportunities they're looking for what psychologist Frederick Herzberg calls "motivators." These motivators include:

- The opportunity to pursue fulfillment through additional research opportunities
- The opportunity to pursue new knowledge
- The opportunity for recognition and status and other things that drive people to excel

By contrast, what he calls "hygiene factors" are those that relate to the level of wages, job security, and safe working conditions. They're not as powerful an incentive for passion-driven workers, who are the primary source of brain drain. The nations that best facilitate and support these pursuits tend to attract specialists away from nations that restrict the same pursuits.

Why You Should Care

Brain drain results in lower levels of development, innovation, and decreased competitiveness in the international markets. In the long run it will lead to a slowing or complete stagnation of the national economy. The lack of experienced or skilled perspectives will reduce the ability of sectors to anticipate or respond to market dynamics, and tends to limit improvements in social or political influences.

80. TAX MANAGEMENT

One variable of which investors and business executives are acutely aware when deciding in what country to allocate their assets is a nation's tax policies. There are hundreds of different taxes that can be levied on money earned within a nation, money earned outside the home nation, money moved between nations, assets owned in a nation, and on any work that is done that adds value to a product. The taxes levied by governments on people, businesses, or assets all influence the movement of capital across international borders.

For instance: PaperCup, Inc. manufactures paper cups in both Freedonia and Brungaria and exports those paper cups to nations all around the world. Freedonia raises its income tax to 50 percent, cutting the income that PaperCup, Inc., makes after taxes. So the company drops production in Freedonia and shifts the majority of its production assets to Brungaria.

The change in the tax rates between two nations gave PaperCup, Inc. an incentive to change which nation it did business in. This incentive comes from a calculable decrease in tax burden that will result in changing the nation in which these assets are held.

This isn't tax management, exactly, though. Tax management is the process by which company management decides how to reduce the organization's tax burden. Through the process of tax management, assets move in response to changes in tax policy. If it becomes generalized among a number of firms, this can be a factor, of course, in creating capital flight.

What You Should Know

Taxes influence not only the distribution of international assets and production, but also the trade that occurs around the world. Every nation taxes imports from other nations differently. So relative differences in tax rates not only influence where assets are held but between which nations exchanges will take place and in which nation those transactions will take place.

Sometimes the availability of suppliers or customers is so significant in a nation that it's worth it for the company to operate there in spite of the higher tax rate. A nation might provide services to employees such as free health care, which would be more expensive for the company to provide than the cost of the higher taxes. As with everything, it's a question of cost-benefit analysis.

Sometimes it's possible to get the best of all worlds. For instance, if your nation has a 10 percent import tariff on ice cubes from Antarctica, it might be possible to find a third-party intermediary located in a nation that has no tariff. Ice cubes from Antarctica are exported to an import/export company in Brungaria, which has no tariff on ice cubes. Your company then imports from Brungaria, circumventing the tariff entirely and without incurring the costs of relocating elsewhere for the purpose of importing ice cubes from Antarctica.

Why You Should Care

Tax management decisions are not exclusive to large multinational organizations that hold assets in multiple nations. If you're a typical small investor, you have access to international markets with varying tax policies that can influence your returns on investment. Even the goods that you buy come from different nations and so can be influenced by tax policy. If you work in multiple nations, the taxes you pay compared to the services you receive can play a role in your decision to either accept a job or go to school in that nation. Whether any of this is a good or a bad thing really depends on what you're trying to do. All other things being equal, though, people will seek out a location for their trade and resources with the lowest possible tax burden.

81. TRANSFER PRICING

Transfer pricing is the process by which an organization attributes a price to its assets that are being transferred between its different divisions. It provides data that helps a company decide whether to outsource services as well as to determine the profitability of various divisions.

Transfer pricing is usually applied to inventories or works in progress. The unfinished product is given a fair market price, given its production costs up until that point as well as the price for similar unfinished products in the market. Then the company's different divisions "purchase" that unfinished product from other divisions. Although no cash actually changes hands, this provides an outline for the costs and added values that can be attributed to each division within a company as a single item is transferred between the separate divisions.

While this process, by itself, provides important information about the financial and operating efficiencies of the organization, when applied to global economics there are some important implications tied to this process for purposes of taxes, outsourcing, and the relocation of operations within a single organization. The information derived from transfer pricing contributes to important decisions, including trade production, employment, tax revenues, investments, and much more.

What You Should Know
The price that organizations place on their assets being transferred between foreign divisions determines the rate at which those assets are taxed. Often full tariffs are suspended in those cases where the assets are transferred back to the original location after being worked on. Instead an organization may just be charged a value-added tax (VAT), which is a tax on the portion

of the increased value of the assets as measured by the difference between the original transfer price and the transfer price going back. Let's look at a quick example:

- **Step 1:** Alpaca wool from a branch at Company A in Chile is transferred to Ecuador for USD10 per unit, because that's what the company could sell it for on the market.
- **Step 2:** The alpaca wool is spun into yarn in the Ecuadorian branch of Company A.
- **Step 3:** The yarn is transferred back to the Chilean branch at USD11 per unit.
- **Step 4:** The added value is USD1 per unit, so that's what Company A will be taxed on.

Note that in real life, the tax rate depends on the tax policies between nations. Our example explains how added value works; it also shows that profits are not a motive in transfer pricing. The reason for this is that only the end product generates profit. When the company's using transfer pricing to determine whether or not to outsource goods, it wants the most competitive pricing available.

That brings us to the second primary use for transfer pricing: the decision to outsource. When a company knows the transfer price for each of the steps of production, it can more accurately determine whether to outsource any process. If an external organization can provide the value added to a piece of inventory at any step in the production process more cheaply than the company can provide internally, then the company will probably outsource that operation.

Why You Should Care

If you've ever wondered how an organization decides whether to move its assets, operations, branches, or jobs across international boundaries, now you understand a very important step in that decision making. It should be obvious how the decision to move operations can influence that company's employees, the costs that a company incurs as well as the prices it charges as a result, and even the trade in both nations.

82. INTERNATIONAL LOGISTICS

The details underlying international transactions contribute greatly to the feasibility of capital movement, the costs associated with trade, and the risks associated with global economics. Understanding the process by which these transactions actually take place and by which things actually move is key to global economics; we're out of the realm of theory here and have both feet firmly on the ground.

This particular issue is broken down into a series of steps, and problems are frequently encountered when fulfilling those steps. It's much simpler than many suspect, and outlining the steps should help take some of the mystery out of the process of trading and transferring goods worldwide.

What You Should Know

- **Step 1:** The buyer and seller draw up a contract for the purchase/sale of goods. Nothing too complicated here.
- **Step 2:** The buyer's bank gives the seller a letter of credit that ensures the payment of the agreed-upon price.

Basically this works just like an IOU: The bank promises that the buyer has money available and that money will be transferred to the seller upon proof that the shipment has been made.

- **Step 3:** The seller consigns goods to the shipper and is given a bill of lading. The shipper is nothing more, usually, than the national postal service or some shipping company such as FedEx or UPS. The bill of lading includes information about the contents of the shipment, value, destination, and everything else. The seller keeps his portion, a portion goes on the shipment, and the post office gets a copy as well.
- **Step 4:** The seller gives the bill of lading to his bank. The seller's bank then contacts the buyer's bank for the cash transfer.
- **Step 5:** The shipper delivers the goods to the buyer.

Why all these steps? Their object is to create paperwork to track the shipments and make sure everyone stays honest. In lieu of using banks as the third parties, some companies act exclusively as middlemen in these transactions. For a percentage of the transaction value, they will hold onto the shipment until payment is received and then transfer the money to the seller and the goods to the buyer.

Almost all shippers have different options, but there is usually a trade-off between speed and security, and cost. Air shipping tends to be the most expensive but also the fastest and most secure. Shipping by boat tends to be the cheapest but also the slowest and riskiest.

Why You Should Care

Since trade and transfers are within the reach of everyone, a familiarity with the process not only makes it much easier to participate, but helps open doors so you can benefit more from the ability to trade and transfer. For small businesses, which can most greatly benefit from trade but frequently aren't aware that these options are available, an understanding of international logistics can greatly expand their market base as well as make available cheaper sources of supplies.

83. INCOTERMS

International commercial terms, or incoterms, are the terms used in a contract to determine who is responsible for executing certain aspects of shipping, who is responsible for paying for certain aspects of shipping, and at what point responsibility and accountability of a shipment changes hands. Particularly when they include third-party shipping, storage, or distribution, understanding their usage can not only greatly reduce the amount of confusion should something go wrong, but it can also reduce the amount of risk associated with the shipping process.

What You Should Know

Here are some of the most common incoterms. Should ownership change hands in the process of using an intermediary in the shipping process, there will be several legs of the journey, all with various incoterms but not necessarily separate contracts (one contract can include several legs of shipping).

- EXW (Ex works): The buyer is responsible for all aspects of the shipment once it leaves its point of origin.
- FCA (Free carrier): The seller hands over the goods, cleared for export, for disposal by the first carrier (named

by the buyer) at the named place. The seller pays for carriage to the named point of delivery, and risk passes when the goods are handed over to the first carrier.

- FAS (Free alongside ship): The seller must place the goods alongside the ship at the named port. The seller must clear the goods for export.
- FOB (Free on board): The seller must load the goods on board the vessel nominated by the buyer. Cost and risk are divided when the goods are actually on board the vessel. The seller must clear the goods for export. The buyer must instruct the seller about the details of the vessel and the port where the goods are to be loaded, and there is no reference to, or provision for, the use of a carrier or forwarder.
- CFR (Cost and freight): The seller must pay the costs and freight to bring the goods to the port of destination. However, risk is transferred to the buyer once the goods are loaded on the vessel.
- CIF (Cost, insurance, and freight): The seller must pay the costs and freight to bring the goods to the port of destination. However, risk is transferred to the buyer once the goods are loaded on the vessel but the seller pays for the insurance.
- DAT (Delivered at terminal): The seller pays for carriage to the terminal, except for costs related to import clearance, and assumes all risks up to the point that the goods are unloaded at the terminal.
- DAP (Delivered at place): The seller is responsible for the costs of the shipment except customs and tariffs; ownership changes hands to the buyer once the package reaches the first carrier, as does the risk of the shipment.
- CPT (Carriage paid to): The seller is responsible for all aspects of the shipment except customs, tariffs, and insurance.

- CIP (Carriage and insurance paid to): The seller is responsible for all aspects of the shipment except customs clearance and tariffs. This is the same as CPT except that risk continues to stay in the hands of the seller rather than changing hands at the first carrier.
- DDP (Delivered duty paid): The seller is responsible for all aspects of the shipment until it is received by the buyer.

Why You Should Care

Understanding, or at least being familiar with, the terms of a shipping contract can be a great benefit for any large or valuable shipment. If you don't understand anything about it, the process of shipping can hold just as much risk of loss as transaction risk—perhaps more. It is not uncommon for agreements to be made between companies and various intermediaries, forming agreements to increase revenues by referring shipments paid for by the other party to specific carriers. On the other hand, understanding the risks of shipping and including terms to reduce those risks can be critical. Even in recent years, for example, the world has seen an increase in the activities of pirates off the coasts of Africa. If your shipment is stolen, who is responsible for the loss? Who pays for the insurance? Such information should be included in the contract. Unless you know that such options are available to you and what to look for, you may wind up assuming the risk.

CHAPTER 9

Integration

As our understanding of economics has improved over the years, governments have become aware that facilitating free trade between nations is greatly beneficial. True, they often fall back into the trap of trade restrictions and protectionist policies, but on the whole the world is moving toward greater economic integration.

In Chapter 5 we discussed the burdens of trade restrictions. Here we'll go in the opposite direction, toward fewer restrictions and greater integration. As multiple nations become highly integrated they form trade blocs. These amorphous entities sometimes span entire continents or multiple continents and unite different governments under a single economy. The role these trade blocs play in the global economy, their influence over and by their member nations, and whether or not they're beneficial are all issues of considerable debate.

There are trade-offs associated with integration. Increasing national integration improves economic growth and development but reduces each government's ability to act unilaterally. Of course, none of this is new; we live in an increasingly integrated world. But this is having an increasing effect on government policies.

84. FREE TRADE ZONES

The most limited forms of trade integration are free trade zones. These are designated areas within an otherwise closed nation in which free trade is allowed. Imports in the form of raw materials come in, are transformed into manufactured goods, and are exported tax-free and without government intervention (except, of course, for things that directly affect national defense, such as weaponry and other sensitive equipment). Goods for consumption can enter the free trade zone but are not allowed to leave.

Free trade zones can exist in cooperation between any two nations. Sometimes the term "zone" doesn't refer to a specific geographic location but to a type of business. In Mexico, for instance, businesses called *maquiladoras* are allowed to operate in a manner similar to free trade zones. They import raw material to produce manufactured exports with lower trade restrictions than other industries.

Since these free trade zones are designed for the import of raw materials to be processed into manufactured goods, they naturally attract factories and other manufacturing facilities. This has both benefits and detriments—lax regulations on trade and operations can be effective at attracting investment and employment, but they also attract companies and industries seeking to bend rules.

Free trade zones are usually set up in two types of locations: underdeveloped regions and port regions.

- When established in **underdeveloped regions**, the investment and production that the new and improved trade policies attract help develop the area. Companies create jobs, increase the nation's production output, and increase gains from trade and wealth in the area, stimulating development for a higher quality of life. At least that's the theory. The reason that free trade zones are established near **ports** is a little bit less complicated: They're very close to the shipping points through which raw materials will be imported and manufactured products exported.

Since ports and waterways naturally attract trade and industrialization, those organizations that operate there tend to be held to a higher standard for operations and working conditions. These are located in near proximity to other employers; consequently competition for workers is a bit higher since workers have more options and more ability to negotiate for total income. On the other hand, organizations in undeveloped areas, which have few other companies to which workers might apply, have greater negotiating power since the workers have few other choices of employment. This often results in poorer working conditions.

There are free trade zones in many nations on every continent except Antarctica. Some of the more common industries attracted to these regions are electronics, textiles, chemicals, machining, assembly, consumer plastic products, and other products that utilize a high proportion of low- or medium-skilled labor.

What You Should Know

The argument that free trade zones are harmful is a bit misguided. The zones themselves don't do any damage, but the companies that intentionally seek out locations that they believe will not have regulatory oversight for social or environmental impact are damaging. For the sake of this chapter, we'll discuss the economics of free trade zones under the assumption that companies in them are operating within the parameters of the law and that the law is being enforced.

Free trade zones increase the benefits from trade and improve economic ties between nations without much of the generalized codependence inherent with other forms of economic integration. This not only allows a nation to direct investment and trade to the regions it deems strategically important for the management of economic production and growth, but also allows nations to benefit from trade.

Why You Should Care

The opportunities present in free trade areas attract manufacturing and assembly companies that focus on foreign markets. For people, investors, and entrepreneurs within such a nation, they can help direct decision making about the movement of people or capital, while for foreigners the establishment of a free trade zone can help decrease costs. A free trade zone can change the economic dynamics of a nation.

85. PREFERENTIAL TRADE AREA

Preferential trade areas, or preferential trade agreements, are far more common than free trade zones but less broad in their removal of trade restrictions. These are agreements between two or more nations that reduce the amount of trade restrictions between them, but often only marginally. A preferential trade area covers all the nations that are part of the agreement. The limitations on trade restrictions between nations apply to the entirety of both nations; however, they only apply to those nations that are a part of the agreement. Any trade restrictions that a nation had established prior to signing the preferential trade agreement still apply to all countries not a part of the agreement.

The goal of a preferential trade area is to reduce but not eliminate trade restrictions. This tends to increase the amount of trade in both goods and services, increase volume of capital moving across the border, and decrease the costs associated with performing these transactions. The establishment of a preferential trade area doesn't commit nations to cooperate regarding economic policies outside the parameters of the agreement.

Preferential trade areas, like many forms of economic integration, tend to spring up between nations that have a close geographic proximity to each other. This proximity makes the economic impact of trade restrictions more easily viewable, and it's easier to see the benefits of freer trade. As globalization increases, however, and the amount of international exposure between nations increases, agreements between geographically and politically disparate nations are increasing.

What You Should Know

There are a large number of preferential trade areas. For instance:

- The Latin American Integration Association has fourteen member nations in Central and South America
- The Asia-Pacific Trade Agreement has seven member nations along Asia's southern ridge
- The South Asian Free Trade Area has eight member nations along the border between Asia and the Middle East

There are a great number of these sorts of agreements; some are made between just two nations, giving each other preferential status without other nations getting involved. In addition, a single nation can belong to many different preferential trade areas; it can treat different nations with different sets of policies depending on which agreement it is a party to, if it is a party to any agreement at all.

Not all preferential trade areas have exactly the same terms of agreement. The only prerequisite for an agreement to provide preferential trade status between nations is that it reduces the amount of trade restrictions for goods, services, and/or capital. The agreement does not have to eliminate any restrictions entirely, nor does it have to provide any specifics about the types of restrictions being reduced or the amount of reductions being made. As long as there is some preferential status in trade being given to the nations in agreement but not necessarily to other nations, and the reductions in trade restrictions are not so great that the area should qualify to be labeled with some stronger form of economic integration, it is considered a preferential trade area.

Why You Should Care

Since each preferential trade area has its own rules by which the member nations must abide, the impact that each trade agreement has will vary from area to area. Will a particular preferential treatment help a particular sector, location, or business? It's impossible to say without first reading the details of the agreement in question. So, if there is no set of standard benefits to a preferential trade area, why should you care? Well, generally speaking, even if the terms to a preferential trade area don't directly impact you, the economy as a whole still benefits by increasing resource efficiency, decreasing costs, and all the other good stuff that comes with trade.

86. FREE TRADE AREA

In a free trade area, all trade restrictions are eliminated. Those nations party to a free trade area don't have any tariffs, quotas, export subsidies, or any other restrictions on the movement of goods, services, or capital between nations.

This does not mean, however, that people can move freely between the nations, although a certain degree of freedom and expediency in the movement of people is often a requirement for making the movement of goods and capital efficient. Simply put, if a truck driver can't cross the border, then the shipment he's driving can't cross the border, either.

The other primary feature of a free trade area is that each nation is still allowed to set its own economic policies not related to the free trade agreement without coming to a consensus with the other member nations. Unfortunately, this can cause a conflict of interest in trade. For instance, if Freedonia wants to place a tariff on Sylvania, but Brungaria does not want the same tariff on Sylvania, Freedonia and Sylvania may join as a free trade area. In that case goods from Sylvania can enter Freedonia duty-free by using Brungaria as an intermediary through which the goods are imported and then distributed throughout the free trade area.

What You Should Know

As with preferential trade areas, there are a large number of free trade areas that are based on geographic proximity between the member nations. Perhaps one of the most well known of these free trade areas, and certainly the most widely recognized, is the North American Free Trade Agreement (NAFTA). This is an agreement between the nations of Canada, the United States, and Mexico and is one of the largest single trade blocs in the world, as measured by GDP of the member nations as well as the volume and value of capital moved across the borders.

The implementation of NAFTA in 1994 meant that over the course of fifteen years, all tariffs and quotas on any goods, services, or capital being traded or otherwise moved between the three member nations were eliminated. Some restrictions, however, remained. For example, the United States has a full embargo on all goods from Cuba, so although goods from Cuba can be found in both Mexico and Canada, they do not enter the borders of the United States, regardless of the fact that they're passing through a nation party to NAFTA.

Why You Should Care

It is at this level of economic integration that we see the economies of countries rearrange themselves to their optimal balance of production and trade. For example, after passing NAFTA, many parts of the United States went through a process of deindustrialization: A large amount of capital and industrial production left the nation because it could be performed more efficiently in either Canada or Mexico. The trade restrictions for the member nations of a free trade agreement are so low that the natural equilibrium of economic forces reaches their optimal balance. In other words, companies and people are free to search between the nations of a free trade area for options to relocate their businesses, outsource production, purchase supplies, sell their goods, make investments, and all other forms of economic transactions, so that the amount of supply and demand for trade between nations and the amount of output that each nation produces change to a significant degree. Basically, people and companies are free to respond to normal economic pressures as is most effective without government intervention.

While this process is greatly beneficial in the long run, it is not always comfortable. It leads to the movement of people across borders, changing demographics of capital ownership in each nation (i.e., fears of majority foreign ownership), and the movement of unwanted goods such as drugs or weapons. Still, these are all events that occur already.

87. CUSTOMS UNION

When a trade bloc has all the traits of a free trade area but then goes a step further to unify and coordinate the trade policies of all member nations, it becomes a customs union. In other words, all the nations collaborate to form a single set of trade policies adhered to by all the members. The first requirement is that all trade must be free of restrictions in the same manner as a free trade area. The second requirement is that all the member nations treat other nations in the same way.

Since customs unions set their own domestic economic and trade policies, nations tend to be far less enthusiastic about joining a customs union, and there are far fewer active customs unions than there are free trade areas. This degree of political integration begins to reduce the amount of sovereign control that a nation has over its own policies. Governments tend to resent having to reach a consensus with other governments before taking action.

What You Should Know

Those trade blocs that are customs unions, without involvement or overlap with more integrated trade blocs, are established among those nations with smaller and more volatile economies. The two most successful and longest-living customs unions, CAN and Mercosur, are South American. CAN is the Andean Community, the oldest and currently the largest distinct customs union with a total of thirteen members (four full members and several outside members through alternative agreements between those nations and CAN, called associate members). Mercosur is a bit newer and smaller with only nine member nations (three full members, five associate members, and one member, Paraguay, currently suspended for political problems). In Africa, the EAC (East African Community) is similar to CAN in structure.

Customs unions tend to consist of nations with very small or volatile economies because these clusters of nations united by proximity will cooperate with each other for mutual benefit, particularly regarding international political and economic relations. They have similar cultures and similar goals, which allows them to work together effectively. By forming a customs union, these nations gain greater influence, negotiating power, and a more unified message than any member nation could hope to accomplish on its own.

In 2005 the members of Mercosur joined CAN as "associate members." Mercosur is still its own entity but its coordination with CAN continues. These two groups, rather than attempting to position themselves relative to each other, found that they have similar goals and have begun working together, providing even greater international synergy through cooperation and coordination of the economic policies and efforts of their member nations.

Why You Should Care

Customs unions must be looked at as a single agglomerative entity rather than a collection of individual member nations, as is the case with free trade areas. It's not that these nations have merged to form a single large nation; each member nation is still run by a sovereign government that maintains nearly the same amount of control over domestic and international policy. However, despite the friction that may occur within the customs union in deciding trade policy, the policies that form will be consistent across all member nations. The nations become more interdependent on each other, working as pieces of a large economic machine rather than smaller, separate machines.

88. COMMON MARKET

Those trade blocs that allow for the free exchange not only of trade and the movement of capital across international borders, but also the free movement of people, are considered common markets. This degree of freedom for all the factors of production to move between nations forms—for the purposes of asset allocation and, to a large extent, trade with outside nations— a single nation. Although the establishment of a unified set of policies regarding trade with nonmember nations is not a prerequisite for a common market, its tendency to become a single integrated economic entity often has this end result.

What You Should Know

Currently the only trade bloc that is a common market is the South Asian Free Trade Area (SAFTA), which includes a number of nations along the southern parts of Asia and the Middle East. Other common markets, though, provide better insight into the advantages and disadvantages of this type of economic formation. For instance, Canada established a common market for its various provinces in 1995. The individual provinces in Canada are given a large degree of autonomy, and the establishment of a common market among them helped to improve national cohesion and unity among the separate regions of a single country. Across the Atlantic Ocean, several nations in northern Europe established a common market called the European Economic Area (EEA), which allows them to participate in the European Union trade bloc without becoming even more integrated.

Why You Should Care

Common markets are the most economically integrated form a trade bloc can take without actually requiring a consensus between nations about setting economic policies. These markets sometimes have similar, if limited, policies on trade with nonmember nations. Several trade blocs of lower integration have the goal of eventually reaching the status of a common market because of the perceived benefits associated with increasing free trade integration while maintaining a high degree of political independence.

89. ECONOMIC UNION

The next step in achieving total economic integration is the formation of an economic union. This entity combines the traits of common markets and customs unions. An economic union not only allows for the free exchange and movement of goods, capital, and people across the borders of the member nations without restriction, but it also develops a single, common set of policies regarding economic relations with nations that are not members of the economic union. However, members of the union maintain their individual fiscal and monetary policies. Each nation continues to set its own policies for taxation and expenditures, and for the value and quantity of money and interest rates. This allows them to appropriately respond to the dynamics of global economics in order to optimize their own economic potential. At the same time, they present a united set of foreign economic policies consistent with the rest of the economic union.

What You Should Know

Members of an economic union gradually transition to a unified set of foreign trade policies. After this transition phase, the members are fully integrated into the union. Internally there is almost no difference between an economic union and a common market. Economic unions simply take that additional step to formalize the interdependent economic relationship that exists between its members. But even if there's little practical difference, there are large cultural and political obstacles in the way of such a union. Many nations prefer to remain independent and ferociously individualistic.

Why You Should Care

Right now there are no multilateral trade blocs that can be called economic unions. Most either fall into the category of monetary unions or common markets. Still, there are a few bilateral agreements that come close to the description. Other less-integrated trade blocs intend to continue integrating until they become an economic union. These formations and their functioning will soon be very important for trade, particularly in developing nations in South America, Africa, and South Asia.

90. MONETARY UNION

Short of merging multiple nations into a single nation, the formation of a monetary union is as integrated as different national economies can become. There are only two monetary unions in the world: the European Union and CARICOM.

1. CARICOM (Caribbean Community) is a monetary union consisting of twenty-seven nations, mostly small island countries in the Caribbean but also with a handful of nations from Central and South America.
2. The European Union (EU) is a monetary union with several special unique traits; it will be discussed in greater detail later in this chapter.

In addition to maintaining the free exchange of trade, capital, and people across international borders, and maintaining a single set of economic policies regarding trade and capital movement with nonmember nations, monetary unions go one step further and create a centralized body for the management of unified fiscal and monetary policy. In other words, all the member nations become, for economic purposes, one nation. While each nation does maintain a certain degree of control over its fiscal policy (taxation and government spending), it must be aligned with all other countries in the union as well as the goals of the monetary union as a whole. This presents a question: how integrated is too integrated? That is to say, at what point does the level of integration that nations agree to become a hindrance?

What You Should Know

Throughout this book I've advocated free trade, but monetary unions, by integrating large numbers of nations with such widely different economies, can create problems as well. Nations need the ability to adapt.

Let's take the expansion of monetary unions to their logical extreme: the full economic integration of all nations on earth under a single currency and a single monetary policy. The vast and ever-changing differences between nations require them to be able to respond by changing the value of their currencies, inflation rates, monetary and fiscal policies, and other policies, both domestic and international. With continued integration across a greater number of nations, governments lose the ability to alter exchange rates, to manage inflation and unemployment rates, or to respond properly to any change in economic status between two nations. Simply put, members of a monetary union must be very confident that their goals and economic cycles are aligned. Otherwise the international economic pressures that they normally experience will cause severe problems.

The issues experienced by monetary unions are the same as those experienced by many nations managing their own internal economic issues. One problem lies in their attempt to balance centralized control over economic and trade policies with the fiscal policies set by the regional and local governments. The needs of individual states/provinces/districts can be extremely difficult to manage when governments must also be responsive to the needs of the nation as a whole. Of course this isn't impossible, but the struggles countries face are not so different from those experienced by monetary unions.

Why You Should Care

The effectiveness of monetary unions has come under heavy debate in recent years. The benefits of economic cohesion between different parts of the same economic body are very well established and can be directly seen as we look around our nation. Without the cooperation between these individual parts of a single country, the discord would cause a large amount of economic inefficiencies.

Critics of monetary unions became more vocal after the 2007 global financial collapse. However, all the nations experiencing economic difficulties as a result of the recession would have been harmed whether they were members of a trade bloc or not. Membership within the trade bloc will allow them, in the long run, to more greatly benefit if they can learn to effectively manage the differentials in local and bloc-wide economic responses.

Conflict of interest within a monetary union is caused by the attempts to use a single set of monetary and fiscal policies. The people of Portugal can have very different needs than the people of Finland. While they both benefit from free trade, the requirement of coordinating a single currency or set of policies can be quite difficult.

91. INVOLUNTARY INTEGRATION

Not all economic integration happens as the result of planned or voluntary agreements between nations. Through increased globalization, markets and outputs spread across international borders regardless of any policies. These trends are completely beyond the control of individuals, companies, or even governments.

Probably the best example of trade that continues despite the massive efforts by governments around the world is the drug trade. The ugly truth is that it will continue, no matter what the governments of the world do to try to stop it. If there are people willing to pay money for a product, then there will always be someone willing to provide it. The illegal drug trade, one of the biggest industries in the world, integrates the globe whether we like it or not.

Another example of involuntary economic integration involves the Internet. The Internet allows exchanges in goods and services to occur regardless of trade restrictions that may already be in place. It allows people to easily circumvent trade restrictions or external economic policies.

What You Should Know

Many nations have tried to increase trade restrictions and move toward protectionist policies that limit both economic and social activities within their borders in an attempt to control the different forms of involuntary integration. Often, these forms of integration are harmful or unwanted—at the very least they're uncontrollable. Countries can only manage them.

As is the case in the drug trade and Internet exchanges, in the era of modern globalization the more restrictions that are placed on trade, the more—paradoxically—we move toward an integrated system that ignores trade restrictions.

Why You Should Care

No matter where you live, your country is in the process of increasing the amount of economic integration it has with neighboring countries as well as nations on the other side of the globe. As with any form of economic integration, the free exchange of capital and ideas without government intervention tends to be beneficial. So in the long run, integration is in your best interests.

92. EUROPEAN UNION

The European Union is a special type of monetary union. First established in 1958 as a less integrated and much smaller trade bloc consisting of six nations, the EU has continuously increased its degree of integration as well as its size. Currently it is the most integrated trade bloc in the world with twenty-seven member nations. The EU is also the biggest economy in the world, surpassing the United States by the equivalent of $2 trillion in GDP.

The European Union is a full monetary union working under a single set of monetary policies and using a single currency (the euro); a single set of fiscal policies, which are given a certain amount of delegation to the member nations; a single set of trade policies; and a freedom of trade and movement across the borders of member nations. All this binds the entire region into a single organized economic entity. The European Union has also taken steps that integrate political control as well as economic control. The individual member nations still maintain the vast majority of political control, including all issues not specifically referred to in the treaties set by the European Union, but they have an established political body, including a parliament, council, court system, and central bank, all designed to undertake those cross-border issues in addition to a specific set of intra-national issues, called competencies.

What You Should Know

The EU is the largest and most broadly reaching attempt at economic integration in modern history. As a result, there is much we can learn from it about economic integration.

Many nations initially resisted or had questions about joining the EU. Some viewed it as an opportunity for smaller and less developed nations to benefit at the cost of more developed nations. Certainly the process of economic reorganization was not an easy one; the locations of specific companies and even entire industries shifted.

Another issue has been the problem with establishing a single currency, a single set of monetary policies, and a unified set of laws regarding fiscal policy and business regulation. As members of the EU, these countries not only use a single currency but they also give up control over monetary policy and a large portion of fiscal and trade policy. So, rather than being able to properly respond as a fully sovereign nation would to global economic pressures, EU nations have, at times, experienced negative consequences that result from not being able to fully manage their own economy.

Does that mean that EU membership is a bad thing? No, since the member nations will experience long-term benefits that exceed the costs associated with a lack of economic responsiveness. Still, the problems persist and those opponents of EU membership are louder than ever.

Why You Should Care

There is still a lot of controversy surrounding the EU, particularly following the 2007 financial collapse, and many nations are giving serious consideration to leaving the union or at least eliminating the use of the euro as a form of currency. The success or failure of the EU will not only have a large impact on the economies of the entire world, but will also shape future attempts at international integration.

CHAPTER 10

Development

This book began by explaining the motivations behind globalization, trade, and the exchanges and interactions that make up the global economic systems. In this, the final chapter, we will discuss the consequences of trade and global economic exchanges. We will talk about what happens as a direct result of global economic interactions and increased globalization, what the gains from trade look like on a global scale, and what happens when trade occurs.

93. GROWTH

The growth of population requires additional production to sustain it while also providing additional workers who contribute to that production. Companies increase in size as they profit from production, reinvest their profits in expanding operations and new technologies, and increase their total production potential. These are the drivers of something called economic growth.

Economic growth refers to the total change in production. There are several ways to measure the value of a nation's production, which we can then use to measure growth.

- **Gross domestic product** (GDP) is the most common measure of growth. GDP measures the market value of all the output that is produced within a nation in a given year. That can be production by foreign-owned organizations within a nation; for example, there are companies owned by foreigners operating in Germany, but that doesn't matter in terms of Germany's GDP because it measures all production within the country's borders.

- The other primary measurement for growth is **gross national product** (GNP), which measures the value of all the output produced by organizations owned by citizens of a single nation. For example, Germany's GNP would be calculated by measuring the value of output by all German-owned companies regardless of where they're located. GDP and GNP aren't growth measures; they're just the measure of the value of total output. A nation's growth is determined by measuring the *rate of change* in the GDP or GNP. If a nation's production is increasing, then the nation's economy is growing. If a nation's production is decreasing, then the nation's economy is contracting.

What You Should Know

In global economics we talk about the relative growth between nations, which leaves us in a bit of a quandary regarding how to measure the value of production. We know from discussing currency in Chapter 4 that, for example, the same apple grown in different countries will have a different value depending on the exchange rate and purchasing power of the domestic currency in each nation. In order to compare growth rates between nations we need to adjust for both currency values in order to "compare apples to apples" (pun fully intended).

We have two apples of the exact same type, size, and weight; one of the apples is grown in Canada, and the other in Romania. The apple from Canada is worth CAD1 and the one from Romania is worth EUR2. Not only does the exchange rate between the

CAD and EUR influence the value of that apple, but so does the purchasing power parity (PPP). So what we do first is convert everything to a single currency. Assuming that the exchange rate is CAD1 = EUR2, then the apple in both nations costs CAD1. In this particular example we'll say that PPP between the two nations is 1 to 1, so no further adjustments are needed. If the PPP between the two nations was different we'd also have to adjust for Romania's purchasing power to make sure the value of that apple is equivalent for both nations.

We do all this because when we're comparing the total production of two nations, it's not as easy as simply saying that one produced more apples than the other. Canada and Romania produce different things, in different quantities, with different traits. So in order to compare the growth of two nations we adjust for exchange rate to make sure that isn't changing the value of our calculation, then we adjust for PPP. The final number shows which nation is actually producing more or less and by how much.

Why You Should Care

In global economics, knowing which countries are growing faster or slower can help investors to better assess an investment's potential. It can also help nations understand how to allocate their assets and better set their policies, and it helps everyone to better predict what's going to happen within their own nation.

If the value of a nation's total production increases at the same rate as its population growth, then its growth per capita will remain the same. If the value of a nation's production grows more quickly or more slowly than its population, then the growth per capita will increase or decrease. As someone—preferably you—accumulates wealth, he or she can purchase more goods to make their own life more comfortable. This is how increased growth per capita translates to increased quality of life.

94. DEVELOPMENT

Whereas growth seeks to measure the increased wealth available to the people of a nation, development refers to measures of the quality of life. This can be a subjective issue, of course, since people around the world tend to value different things.

Before looking at the metrics for quality of life, we need to define exactly what quality of life is. Quality of life refers to the overall well-being of a nation's people and its communities. Basically, we're looking to estimate whether the people of a nation are happy and secure in their lives. As we measure development, an increase in each metric is meant to indicate an improvement in the quality of life in a nation, while a decrease in the metric is meant to show a lower quality of life.

Several different indices are generally accepted as providing some idea of a nation's quality of life. The most commonly cited is the **Human Development Index** (HDI), which uses a weighted average taking into account measures of health, wealth, and education. Another composite index that uses a more comprehensive set of scores is the **Quality of Life Index** (QLI). This index was established by *The Economist* in 2005 and includes nine different metrics: life expectancy, divorce rate, attendance in community organizations, GDP per person, political stability, climate, unemployment rate, political freedom, and gender equality.

What You Should Know

National economic development is a much more difficult thing to sustain than growth. In fact, most measures of development include GDP per capita as only a single measure in the composite. The remainder comes from the ability of a nation to use the increased wealth to make available to the nation's people a variety of services contributing to their overall standard of living. This means infrastructure development; the distribution of quality medical care and safety services such as police, fire, and military; access to an education (even if that's career training rather than traditional education); environmental renewal infrastructure; and access to utilities.

Generally speaking, increases in wealth tend to lead to increased development. The reason that many nations have large deviations in their levels of development, though, has as much to do with the original sources of economic development as with current modern sources.

Why You Should Care

While economic growth is important, contributing greatly to the lives of a nation's people, the ultimate goal of nations is development. First- and second-world countries are seeking the sustainable industrialization that puts them on the road to becoming developed nations. The development of a nation determines not only the quality of life for its people, but also its future potential. People who have the ability to innovate will improve their nation beyond what was previously possible, but this only happens when they have the knowledge, physical capability, and resources to allocate to such an initiative. As a result, development is what improves the world, while growth only makes development possible.

95. INCOME DISPARITY

We've talked several times now about how people generate wealth from exchanges in goods and services, and how wealth can translate into improvements in national development. But wealth is not distributed equally. In any given nation, some maintain a larger share of wealth than others. This income disparity is measured using the Gini coefficient. This is a number between 0–1 that measures what proportion of people own what proportion of wealth. A Gini coefficient of 0, for example, means that income is distributed evenly across all people; 1 percent of the people own 1 percent of the income, 50 percent of people own 50 percent of the national income, and 99 percent of the people own 99 percent of the income. At the other extreme, a Gini coefficient of 1 means that the total national income is distributed perfectly unevenly; one person owns 100 percent of the income. Of course, in the real world these two extremes are never encountered.

The Gini coefficient is usually expressed through a graph. A straight diagonal line shows the theoretical perfectly equal distribution; a perfectly unequal distribution wouldn't be seen because it just runs along the bottom and far right side of the graph. What's important is the curve illustrating the real national distribution of income, called the Lorenz curve. The further away from the horizontal line that your nation's Lorenz curve gets, the more unequal is your nation's income distribution.

What You Should Know

Whether maintaining an income disparity is a good thing or bad thing has been a matter of heated debate for centuries. It's often led to revolutions and wars, and the exact amount of disparity that is seen as optimal, if any, is a topic that has not been soundly established. The debate comes squarely on two primary issues: ensuring a fair and equitable compensation or incentive system, and the role of investments.

In the first issue, regarding compensation, neither planned economic systems nor market-based systems have truly found an effective answer. Much of the problem appears to be the result of the ability of those who manage capital to retain much greater negotiating power than the labor market (particularly during periods of high competition for jobs, such as during recessions), easily manipulate short-term financial information, and influence politics, regardless of the incentive schemes and amount of control (or lack thereof) established. On the other side of the argument, it is said that the value generated by high-income individuals is higher, and the market responds appropriately. We know this to be false, however, because executive income has increased dramatically even as average corporate financial performance and GDP fall, or otherwise do not increase as quickly as average executive compensation.

Regarding the use of the socioeconomic disparity, perfect equality results in entrepreneurs having fewer resources with which to invest in businesses, innovations, and other economic growth projects. Perfect inequality implies that no one is being properly compensated for their resources. The balance is, of course, found somewhere in the middle.

Why You Should Care

All companies around the world stay in business only because people have the resources to purchase their goods. The socioeconomic disparity is not an ideological issue; it's merely an issue of managing supply and demand. Decreasing the socioeconomic disparity and thereby increasing the amount of money that people have will increase the amount of goods that people want to purchase, increase the number of people that will be taxed, increase total tax revenues, and stimulate growth. Increasing the socioeconomic disparity increases the amount of assets available to invest in a company's search for returns on investment, improving innovation and development. The exact balance is a very careful one to manage, but it is one that is all too often looked at in extreme ideological terms.

96. DEVELOPED AND DEVELOPING NATIONS

In terms of their development, nations are divided into three primary categories: developed, developing, and least developed. Developed and developing nations are not so different from each other, though they're at different phases in their process of modernization. Because of this, we'll consider both these categories together.

The exact criteria by which nations are evaluated to determine whether they're developed or developing is an issue of contention. In many cases it can be quite clear, particularly when comparing a very developed nation like Germany to a much less developed nation such as Romania, which is still struggling to industrialize. The exact point at which a nation changes from developing to developed (or, in unfortunate circumstances, from developed to developing) is not entirely clear, though, as there is no single agreed-upon division. Still, these are all semantics. When looking at the difference between developed and developing nations, what is more helpful is the process of development.

Think of development as a bit like the human life cycle. Developing nations are growing and developing, often very quickly and frequently in an awkward manner during which time the nation struggles to define itself and its role in the greater global context, working to establish a stable economic identity.

Developed nations are those that are considered to be mature. They've reached a point where they no longer rely exclusively on an absolute advantage in the form of cheap labor or the consumption of their natural resources. They've established some industrialization in industries in which they have a comparative advantage, yet they've diversified their economies enough to maintain reasonable economic stability. The growth of their production and income has achieved an easily manageable rate, and they have established an infrastructure consistent with improved quality of life.

What You Should Know

Terms such as "first-world nation" and "third-world nation" are declining in popularity, but they can still be useful. A first-world nation is a developed nation; a second-world nation is developing. There is some criticism regarding the use of the term "developing" nation, since many argue that it implies inferiority. So to clarify: A developing nation is merely one that is at a different stage in its economic development.

The age of a culture or how long a people have been established in a geographic area has no bearing on economic development. The age of a nation can, however, influence the extent to which a society is politically stable, a primary prerequisite to economic development.

Examples of developed nations include Japan, Sweden, Italy, Taiwan, and Britain. Examples of developing nations include China, Brazil, India, Mexico, and the Czech Republic.

Why You Should Care

Understanding the traits of developed and developing nations is important to grasp the role of each nation in the global economy. Businesses and investors look to developing nations as

places in which to expand operations. Developmental economists and government officials look at how developed nations
achieved their status as a guide for how other nations can do
the same. Your exposure to a particular culture or the availability of goods and services from many nations will depend greatly
on whether that nation has reached a point of development in
which sustainable and stable trade can be established.

97. LEAST-DEVELOPED NATIONS

In contrast to developed and developing countries, least-developed nations (LDNs) are those that have not yet begun industrialization or where it is weak and faltering. Often these nations
rely exclusively on the extraction of natural resources (mining, oil,
natural gas, etc.) and subsistence farming (in which the people of
a nation survive by producing their own foods and goods rather
than by trading). LDNs usually have very low (or no) income per
capita, low levels of infrastructure in such areas as transportation
and utilities (much less education and health care), political and
social instability, and economic volatility. These result from the
inability of the nation to begin those processes of capital movement described in Chapter 8.

Industrialization and urbanization tend to occur only
temporarily through projects funded by foreigners. Once the
projects are complete, fledgling cities often experience rapid
growth followed by devastating urban decay. Consider the case
of the Panama Canal. This construction project brought in a
huge number of jobs and increased prosperity within Panama.
Once the canal was complete, though, the jobs disappeared and
the cities built on the wealth of this project quickly sank into
decrepitude.

LDNs are also known as third-world, preindustrial, or agrarian nations. Examples include Madagascar, Nepal, Haiti, Sierra Leone, and North Korea.

What You Should Know

Reasons for the difficulty in development in LDNs generally come from two sources: natural hurdles and national instability. Most of the LDNs in the world suffer from challenges of location. Often they're in places with few inland waterways, low rainfall, a prevalence of deadly diseases such as malaria, or extreme geographic features such as mountainous terrain. National instability refers to not only economic instability, but also social and political instability. LDNs often suffer from a lack of diversification in the nation's industries, leading to severe fluctuations in supply and demand for its goods and leading to dramatic periods of unemployment. This puts a nation's currency at risk of exchange rate fluctuations, contributing to its questionable value as a unit of exchange.

Socially, instability can refer to conflicts between people (usually tribal or religious groups), xenophobia, and decisions based on cultural superstitions. An inability to establish a single government is often the single largest barrier to future attempts at development. This was a huge problem in Myanmar (a.k.a. Burma) for decades, as an oppressive military junta stopped any development from occurring.

Why You Should Care

It is in the world's least-developed nations that we find the greatest amount of economic potential. People around the world have spent an immense amount of resources trying to stimulate sustainable development in these areas. Throughout parts of

Africa one can still find the remains of portions of railroad track where foreign investors, businesses, and nations worked with local people and governments to establish a transportation infrastructure. Burdened by high costs, the dangers of disease, and the risks of local violence, many of these projects were eventually abandoned.

Another unfortunate side effect of the attempts to industrialize many LDNs has been a growth in national debt. Nations are given loans for infrastructure development, and individuals are given loans to start businesses. These loans are economic traps that put people and nations under the control of foreign nations and banks. As a result, these loans often end up harming the development process.

98. THE NORTH-SOUTH GAP

A line has become apparent that separates developed nations from least-developed nations. The equator acts as a sort of informal geographic border that defines the trends in economic growth and development for the nations on either side of it. On the north side of the equator lie the vast majority of developed nations; nations north of the equator tend to have much higher rates of growth and development. South of the equator one finds the vast majority of least-developed nations. This economic variation along equatorial lines is referred to as the North-South Gap, or the North-South Divide.

What You Should Know
The causes of the North-South Gap have been discussed for much of the past century. Needless to say, there was a significant

amount of nonsense in the beginning, some of it related to genetics and race. Today it's generally accepted that the difference is the result of two influences: differences in the original sources of development from prehistoric times, and a lack of growth and trade resulting from those difficulties that leads to the various forms of instability.

We'll discuss the original sources of development in the next topic. For now I'll just say that the natural resources available to people prior to the Bronze Age still play a great role in the degree of development each nation experiences today. A lack of resources resulted in an inability to trade. As people spent all their time working in order to survive, no surpluses could be established with which to trade for other goods. This, in many regions, stopped economic development before it could even begin.

Regarding the second primary source, instability continues to hinder development (see previous). Those people who can afford to do so will go to more developed nations seeking opportunities. This emigration of skill and resources also helps to maintain the divide between global north and global south.

Why You Should Care

On a global scale we are still very far from reaching our total economic potential. There is yet much more we can accomplish in increasing the growth and development of every nation on the planet, even developed nations, by establishing a set course of development among LDNs, particularly in those nations in the global south, which lack the resources or ability to begin the development process. In addition, this inequitable distribution of wealth and development has resulted in a number of human rights concerns that would be best resolved as soon as possible.

99. SOURCES OF DEVELOPMENT

The reason that some nations are economically developed and others are not can be explored by looking at the original sources of development and how they benefited the people of a particular country. Economic development throughout history has relied heavily on the inputs of production. As we discussed in Chapter 1, those nations that find ways to create production in excess of what they will use are able to trade the surplus for other goods; both nations party to the trade will benefit.

Now take that idea of international trade between nations and shrink it down to the trade between communities in a single nation, or even between individuals within a single community. Gains from trade continue to generate wealth as long as they allow participants to produce more together than they could on their own.

Today, thanks to the increased access that people all over the world have to the factors of production, there are a large number of ways to make this happen:

- Sharing of production methods
- Involvement from foreign investors
- Foreign aid
- International corporate expansion

However, the modern distribution of wealth and development around the world is not so different from that of the ancient world. People were originally able to create these sets of circumstances primarily from the natural resources they found around them.

Natural resources differ from country to country; the plants that grow in each, the animals, climate, minerals, physical geography—all are different. It is also possible, though, to find similarities between developed nations and undeveloped nations.

Studying these similarities and differences and their evolution over time contributes to our understanding of economic and social development.

What You Should Know

The pursuit of those products and methods that increase production yields is where development began. When everyone in a community is dedicating all their time to producing food (gathering, hunting, processing, preserving, etc.) to stay alive, people aren't producing tradable surpluses, they aren't producing other types of goods, and they certainly aren't developing. For example, many indigenous people of southern Africa and parts of southeast Asia who rely heavily on palm trees for their food and building supplies find it difficult to accumulate surpluses. The reason is that palm trees are very time-consuming to process into food and building supplies; they also have relatively low nutritional value compared to other crops.

Let's contrast that with a higher-yield product: corn. Like palm trees, nearly every part of the corn plant can also be used, but unlike the palm tree, corn grows much more easily and quickly. It produces more edible material per acre, takes less effort to process, and is more nutritious. As a result, a single person can produce corn for a very large number of people, allowing those other people to dedicate their time and efforts to something other than producing food. The real difference between these two circumstances isn't the knowledge that corn makes better food than palm trees; it's simply that palm trees grow naturally in some areas while corn does not. If palm is the only thing, then you're having palm for dinner. So, plants that grow in a particular area play a large part in the region's development. The same can be said for the animals that are indigenous to different areas.

National geography also plays an important factor. Many nations have a very difficult time developing because of a severe lack of water or waterways. Australia, for example, is developed only around the coasts. Since the continent has no inland waterways that penetrate deep into the interior, the vast majority of the nation is completely undeveloped.

The availability of mined goods within the earth has also been a primary contributor to the origins of development. During the Copper and Iron Ages, people began relying heavily on these metals as a more effective material for tools. Regions that lacked these materials did not make this leap forward.

Why You Should Care

Much of the development experience in the United States occurred when crops and growing methods used by Native Americans were used in combination with the production methods and domesticated animals brought by the European settlers. What this tells us is that stimulating development in nations around the world can produce dramatic results when we understand the process better. However, we must proceed cautiously and learn from past mistakes in this area.

100. URBAN RENEWAL

Urban areas—even entire nations—can be subject to decay and other forms of economic dilapidation, but that's really not the end of the story. Such disaster areas often go through a process of revitalization called urban renewal. This is the process of re-establishing growth and development in a previously decayed area.

The process combines city planning with economic stimulus initiatives. The ultimate goal is threefold:

1. The area must once again attract investments from businesses and entrepreneurs seeking to begin business operations, thereby revitalizing industrialization or postindustrial manufacturing.
2. Any renewal effort must attract individuals by making the city a desirable place either to live in or visit.
3. The city or nation must become economically sustainable and efficient.

These renewal efforts must usually begin early in the phases of decay, while the city is still generating enough revenues to invest in the renewal process. Renewal is a very expensive initiative and if a city waits until the problem gets out of hand, it may not be able to generate enough revenues to pay for it. Detroit, Michigan, is a perfect example of this. Several community-based initiatives have been attempted, but without city support they aren't enough to combat rampant decline.

What You Should Know

The idea of urban renewal is a relatively new one, and many failed experiments have occurred, all with good intentions, of course. Here are some of the more successful projects:

- *Mixed Purpose Districts.* A single district can include commercial, industrial, and residential use. This tends to decrease vehicle traffic by eliminating the need to traverse larger areas to get to your intended location.
- *Mixed Value Housing.* Rather than having upscale housing regions, low-priced districts, and entire neighborhoods

dedicated to subsidized housing, communities should include mixed-value housing. This helps to maintain a more even distribution of revenues and expenditures across an entire city and increases overall community involvement and interaction, improving maintenance rather than forcing low-income areas to fall into decay.

- *Pedestrian-Focused Planning.* Moderate to large areas dedicated to pedestrian traffic decrease vehicle reliance, which in turn decreases pollution and minimizes the need for expensive public transportation, improves accessibility, and increases community involvement and public interaction. This also improves public safety by maintaining a higher proportion of interpersonal communication and accountability.
- *Revitalization.* Public art projects, community-based beautification projects, refurbishing historic/cultural spots, demolishing blighted buildings, and the addition of landmarks such as fountains or statues all help to improve overall morale, decrease crime, and increase community pride.
- *Community Involvement and Safety.* Initiatives for neighborhood watch programs to ensure the safety and security of people minimize flight of population and capital.
- *Public Facilities.* Centrally located parks, public restrooms, public drinking fountains, and other contributions to public spaces are a must. People should feel safe and welcome in them.
- *Freeway Planning.* Ensuring that the city includes both roads and pedestrian areas is critical; freeways should merge into roads by the time they enter the city itself.
- *Geographic Consolidation.* Urban sprawl spreads people out over a much greater geographic area, including multiple different cities and their related suburbs. Consolidating urban

and suburban areas helps to decrease pollution, decrease dependence on vehicles, and maintain a healthy distribution of resources within a single region.

Some of the more successful projects have included efforts to diversify industries within a city, provide tax advantages for organizations that employ larger quantities of people, and facilitate opening new and small businesses. The federal government also gives preference in its contracts to companies that operate out of HUD (Housing and Urban Development) zones.

Why You Should Care

The entire process of urban renewal is to improve a city in order to attract people, businesses, and investors from other regions. The intent is to increase the city's trade gravity to attract production and trade from other areas. Details of city planning and community organization have given important insights into the nature of development itself. By utilizing many of the same methods used by urban renewing planners to drive influxes of investment, production, and population, nations can direct their own planning with the goal of modernizing their nations, starting with individual cities and expanding to other areas.

101. INFLUENCE OF MULTINATIONAL ENTERPRISES

In the twenty-first century, multinational enterprises have an unprecedented amount of influence over the global economy. Each corporation not only maintains command over a much larger value and volume of assets around the world but also has a degree of negotiating power and experience unheard of through-out history. This influence exhibits itself in multiple ways, not all of which are good.

The desire of nations to attract investments and companies for the purpose of stimulating economic growth and development within their nation has led many governments to either neglect or change established laws. Such changes often create poor working conditions, damage to the environment, or poor consumer safety.

For example, many electronics recycling companies in South Asia force their employees to strip toxic but useful metals from old electronics shipped there by foreign companies. The rest of the device is often either burned—releasing toxic chemicals into the air—or dumped into rivers.

What You Should Know

These problematic business practices are not the result of some big conspiracy to destroy humanity. They are the result of poor decision-making that stem from the desire of both businesses and governments to develop themselves, even at the expense of other stakeholders. The decisions are not always easy ones, and some that are considered unethical have benefits that truly are quite valid. Some of these poor scenarios are unethical, but many are simple mistakes.

Why You Should Care

In recent years, companies with business practices that would be deemed unacceptable in their home nations, as well as the foreign governments that do not enforce restrictions against such practices, have come under fire. This has resulted in a number of boycotts, fines and other penalties, and a general increase in corporate social responsibility. It is now considered strategically unfavorable to pursue financial efficiency at the detriment of other stakeholders. Those companies that maintain high-quality, ethical operations, even in foreign nations, are those that experience greater financial performance in the long run.

INDEX